METAL DETECTING FOR BEGINNERS

101 Things I Wish I'd Known When I Started

by M. A. Shafer

A Quickstart Guide

from

An Imprint of Word Forge Books
Riegelsville, Pennsylvania

Metal Detecting For Beginners: 101 Things I Wish I'd Known When I Started
ISBN-10   0-9771329-8-6
ISBN-13   978-0-9771329-8-0

PRINTED IN THE U.S.A.

Published by Sweet Myrrh Books, an imprint of Word Forge Books
5935 Route 412, Suite 6
Riegelsville, PA 18077
610-847-2456

publisher@wordforgebooks.com
http://www.wordforgebooks.com

Learn more about metal detecting for beginners at Detecting101.com and at https://www.facebook.com/MetalDetectingAndTreasureHunting.

DISCLAIMER: Although every effort was made to ensure that the content of this book is accurate and up to date, no part of it should be construed as legal advice. All contents are the opinion and based on the experience of the author, who is not an attorney or legal advisor. All risk associated with following the guidance in this book is borne solely by the reader. Always check local ordinances applying to any location before you metal detect, and observe all laws and restrictions.

Photo credits:

Front cover: Photo by the author. Thanks to Joe and Rikki Montoro for graciously serving as the front cover models.

Back cover: Fotolia.com

p. 21: © Greg Pickens - Fotolia.com

p. 25: Fotolia.com

p. 32: GraphicStock.com

p. 67: GraphicStock.com

p. 100: Photo by D.J. Yost

Contents

For Shelly, who gave me my first metal detector. See what you started?

Foreword

In my opinion, in this wonderful hobby of ours called metal detecting, there is really no such thing as an expert, but there is definitely such a thing as a beginner. Even the most experienced detectorist was once a beginner—we've all been there. Experience is the best teacher. This hobby is ever evolving; the detectorist is always learning.

I remember when I began to take this hobby seriously, back in my early twenties. Trying to research and learn the art of metal detecting was difficult, to say the least. The terminology was frustrating, and even the manual that came with the machine was nearly impossible to read and follow. Most instructions were complex, online sites were scarce, and good resources were hard to come by.

I feel like the book you're about to read is long overdue, and I wish I'd had it when I started detecting. Now there are other books out there for beginners, but this is an essential "pocket guide" to metal detecting. Not only is it handy, it's straight to the point, informational, and—most importantly—easy to understand. This book explains metal detecting in layman's terms and is easy to follow, even for the newest beginner.

To be honest, I've been waiting for Mary to put this project together. I've known her personally for some time now. We met online in the metal detecting community, connected instantly, and formed a genuine friendship.

Watching Mary's progression through the hobby has been amazing. When I first met her, she hadn't even found her first coin yet. Now, six years later, I find great pleasure in watching Mary uncover 200-year-old coins. Through it all, her love for the hobby and willingness to learn sure made her a great digging partner.

She has really come so far from when we first met, and is the perfect person to write this book because she has a way of explaining complex terms so they're easy to understand. I also really like the index, and the fact that this book is so easy to navigate without re-reading the whole book to find what you're looking for.

After reading Mary's book, I have to admit there were a lot of things I'd forgotten about experiencing as a beginner. At one point when I was starting out, I actually thought my machine was broken because I wasn't seeing the same results as other detectorists!

But the basics are a crucial element, no matter which machine you run, or what level detectorist you are. Mary's book speaks to all of us on every level, covering the basics and beyond. It tells you what you need to know without overwhelming you. After reading this book, you should feel more confident even discussing the hobby with others.

This isn't a book that you'll store on your bookshelf. This is one to keep with your gear. The metal detecting community needed this book, and I'm so proud that my friend Mary has now brought it to you.

D.J. Yost
White's Electronics Focus Team Member
Blogger, DJDigs.net
Nazareth, Pennsylvania
March, 2016

Introduction

I've been metal detecting for a dozen years, and the hobby has turned into a real passion for me. When I first got interested, though, it was slow going. I didn't have a clue how to go about the actual detecting, much less actually finding anything. I didn't even know where to start looking. Here I was, all revved up with excitement, and no place to go! It was quite frustrating—a real buzz kill.

I didn't know anyone already into the hobby that I could talk to. I couldn't easily find any information telling how to get started as a detectorist. It was a few years before Facebook became everyone's backyard, and I wasn't familiar enough with the Internet then to know about Special Interest Groups (SIGs) and niche interest websites. So I went where I'd always gone for information: my good ol' public library.

To my disappointment, they didn't have any books about the hobby. They did offer to order a few titles for me through inter-library loan, but the ones they had available were all rather specialized titles. There were books about how to use a certain machine, how to search for certain types of objects, or how to hunt particular types of locations; but there was nothing available simply to help the uninitiated with general how-to information about getting started detecting, from choosing appropriate equipment and finding places to hunt, to the hunt itself and then recovering items once you found them.

Common sense told me there must be legal issues involved in getting permission to hunt on other people's property, but what were they? What kinds of machines were available? What were the important considerations in buying one? What could I expect to pay, and where could buy them? It was too big an investment to make uninformed, so I simply floundered for a few years, my detecting dreams shelved until I could figure it out.

A few years later, I received a beginner's machine for Christmas, and so got started by default. By then, the Internet was pretty well established and I did a search on "metal detecting." I discovered several sites dedicated to the hobby, which offered discussion forums on different topics. I was grateful to find two sites whose forums welcomed newbies and had topic threads just for our ill-informed questions.

To my great relief, there were experienced detectorists on those boards who were kind and patient and welcoming. (I have since found, to my delight, that this characterizes the majority of dedicated diggers.) I took advantage of the ability to ask questions, and made a few friends whom I contacted off the boards and began real friendships with.

Eventually, one of them invited me to a group hunt (thanks, Rikki!), where I got to meet other people from the boards, and that's when my real learning began. There's just nothing like hunting with someone who knows what they're doing to kick your learning into high gear (thanks, Joe!). Then I met D.J. in a metal detecting group on Facebook, found out he lived nearby, and invited him down to hunt my yard with me. And these three folks become my go-to mentors who taught me nearly everything I know. I sure am a lucky gal to have been taken under the wing of these kind and generous people.

These days, there are many websites about metal detecting in all its forms. There are almost as many Facebook pages dedicated to different specialized facets of detecting and treasure hunting. There is even a good book for beginners, but it's a full-length tome that's full of detail and takes some time to get through.

Amazingly, I still haven't found a simple, general "getting started" handbook, one that's basically a collection of tips you can quickly read through and then get out in the field to hunt. *And who really needs one?* you might ask.

Well, I think the answer is probably "many people."

Though I'm a huge fan of the Internet, I don't like doing research on a mobile device, either at home or out in the field, unless I don't have any choice. I'm over fifty, and the teeny print on mobile-optimized websites is just tedious for my older eyes to read.

Maybe I'm a little old-fashioned, but if I want to have a field reference, I still like taking a conveniently sized print book with me. That way, unlike referencing information on a mobile device:

- I can toss it into my gear bag and take it into the field with me, without having to worry about it getting too hot or too cold.

- I don't have to charge it up.

- Using it doesn't depend on being able to get a good cell signal.

- I don't have to be too concerned if it gets a little dirty or dusty or gets a few drops of water on it. I've even had books survive an accidental drop into a mud puddle, which a smartphone almost never will.

- If I do ruin it, I've thrown away less than $10 instead of several hundred.

And so, this book was born. It's a small investment of time and money, intended to help you get started quickly and productively in the hobby, without making potentially expensive or embarrassing mistakes.

I've broken the information out into individual tips you can quickly digest and put into practice, and organized them under related topic headings to help you easily find the information you need. Most folks can get all the way through this book in less than two hours, which is why I call it a Quickstart Guide.

Since my experience is that of an American located in the Lower 48 states, this book references that area. I'm sure most of the points I make here would apply to other countries, with the exception of some issues concerning legal ordinances and statutes, and anything relative to specific machines and accessories, which vary by continent.

This guide does not delve deeply into beach or water detecting, nor gold prospecting. These are all specialized areas of concentration that fall outside the purpose of this beginner's guide, but those who wish to pursue these specialties will still need to learn the material in this book. All of these areas of focus have excellent, comprehensive books written about them, and great online sites that are constantly updated. A quick Internet search should help you find these resources.

To avoid confusion and limiting the usefulness of this information, I've intentionally refrained from mentioning specific brands of equipment, except in areas where it's germane to the functions I'm explaining. There are many companies manufacturing excellent detectors and accessories to make your hunting more successful, and many places to buy these products. You can find them all on the Internet with a quick search, and that information will always be more up-to-date than anything in a book.

Where I have mentioned brand names and functions, it is always based either on my own use of the equipment involved, or on my own direct witnessing of someone else using it. If I mention any malfunction, it is based on repeated instances of this and not on a single issue that could have been a fluke. It is not my intention to call any equipment into question concerning quality, but I do feel it's my duty to be honest about my real experiences.

Use this information in good health, and please let me know what you think. My goal is to make this book as useful as possible to newbies just getting started (and maybe even to those who've been in the hobby a while, but missed some basics along the way). I welcome your feedback so I can fine-tune future editions to be as helpful as they can be.

Good luck, and happy hunting!

Mary A. Shafer, Author
Blogger, Detecting101.com
Bucks County, Pennsylvania
March, 2016

Glossary - Vocabulary & Slang

I recommend you read this section first, as many of the terms here are referenced later in the book.

This is by no means an exhaustive glossary of metal detecting terms. It's intended simply as a starting point, containing the most basic words, phrases and slang terms beginning metal detectorists are most likely to encounter in their first several months or years in the hobby.

You'll certainly hear more terms as you go further into detecting and maybe branch out into other facets of treasure hunting, and as the hobby itself evolves. There are certainly quite a few excellent resources for more terms. But the ones here will get you started and allow you to communicate with other diggers, without having to wonder what they're talking about or feeling stupid (I would have killed to know these terms).

I strongly advocate simply asking when you don't understand a term, instead of pretending you know it and missing out on good information because you have no point of reference. Even if they tease you a little bit, most folks remember when they were newbies and didn't know anything, and will feel good about being able to help you by explaining.

Arm Cuff – The part on the operator's end of a metal detector, usually semi-circular with foam padding, a webbing strap and hook-and-loop closure, intended to secure the machine around the operator's arm. This not only provides control and counter-balance, but also creates a configuration that's comfortable for the user.

Artifacts – Old items of historic interest that may or may not hold monetary value. This tends to be the term used more by historians for found objects. *See Relics.*

Barber – Silver coinage consisting of a dime, quarter, and half dollar, designed by United States Bureau of the Mint Chief Engraver, Charles E. Barber. These were minted between 1892 and 1916, though no half dollars were struck in the final year of the series.

"Beavertails" – *See Pulltabs.*

Beeping – Another name for the act of detecting, referencing the familiar sound most machines make when their coils pass over a target.

"Buff" – Nickname for the Buffalo or Indian Head nickel, minted from 1913-1938. A depiction of the American Bison is on the reverse face of the coin.

Cache – A collection of several to many items, usually intentionally gathered in a single container, and buried for safe-keeping but for one reason or another, never recovered by their original owners. Caches may consist of small jars filled with low-value coins to bags of silver or gold bars, from wood or metal boxes filled with guns and ammo to ancient earthenware vessels filled with hammered Roman coins and jewelry. Though the items contained in caches may not be of much monetary value, finding one is always a thrill.

Can Slaw – Pieces or chunks of tin or aluminum beverage cans; one of the banes of a detectorist's existence. *See Pulltabs.*

Chatter – The annoying, mostly meaningless, non-stop noise made by a detector with its sensitivity turned way up while it's running over mineralized or trashy ground, or in the vicinity of stray electrical signals such as those from overhead wires or underground invisible fences. Ground balancing is supposed to stop it, but this doesn't always work and sometimes you'll have to turn your sensitivity way down or just abandon that spot altogether.

Clad – The name for modern coinage in the U.S., including zinc pennies coated with copper. In 1964, the U.S. Mint began making "silver" coins out of copper sandwiched between—or "clad" in—two layers of silver-colored metal alloy. Before that, higher denomination coins were actually minted from real silver with just a small amount of alloy to harden them. This is called "coin silver" and has a different degree of purity than Sterling Silver, which is .925% pure silver. The only fairly modern coinage not referred to as "clad" are pure copper pennies, which stopped being minted in 1982.

Coil – The part of the metal detector that passes parallel over the ground; usually round or oval-shaped. Double-D is another popular configuration, which gives more depth to the reading. If a target does not pass under your coil, you will never know it's there. "Sniper" coils are the small (usually about 5" in diameter), solid ones that look like hockey pucks, and are used to get in between lots of targets in trashy areas.

Coin Spill – Several coins found very close together, very often in the same hole. Also referred to as a "pocket spill."

Control Box – The part of your metal detector that houses most of the electronics and circuitry that make it work. This part of your machine cannot be allowed to get wet unless your machine is rated waterproof; otherwise, you'll probably ruin the machine. To avoid this, you can cover it with a control box cover from the manufacturer, or a plastic bag will do if you make sure it's tightly closed, but this will protect only from light to moderate rain. You should not operate non-waterproof machines in heavy rain or underwater.

Dateless – A coin that for some reason—usually heavy oxidation, encrustation or heavy use wear—has its date obscured and unable to be read.

Detector – A metal finding machine, generally consisting of an arm cuff, control box, shaft, power cable and coil. Usually requires some type of onboard battery, rechargeable power pack or other power source, and must be swung just over the surface of the ground to operate properly; most detectors won't read a signal if they're not moving over it.

Detectorist – A person who operates a metal detector. Also called a "digger."

Digger – There are two meanings to this word in the hobby. The first is used to describe hobbyists themselves (see above); the term is interchangeable with "detectorist." The second meaning is the handheld tool used to remove earth, sand, stones and other material (sometimes referred to as "overburden," though this term is more applicable to placer gold mining) from the hole where the target is located.

What most folks might call a trowel or hand shovel is a "short-handled digger" and a camp shovel or entrenching tool is a "long-handled digger." It should be noted that diggers designed for metal detecting tend to have MUCH stronger blades that can stand a lot of lever action, and often have one serrated (or "toothed") blade edge.

Eyeball – To discover a relic, coin, nugget or other find with the naked eye, without use of a metal detector: "I eyeballed that quarter just lying on top of the ground."

Falsing – The tendency of some detectors to produce good-sounding signals for trash targets or even non-existent ones. This can happen for any number of reasons and doesn't necessarily indicate a faulty machine, but if your detector constantly produces false signals, you either have to make adjustments to its sensitivity and ground balance, or you might have to get another type of detector for your area's soil conditions.

Finds – All the stuff you find during a hunt. Most people separate the junk out and only consider the keepers "finds."

Foil – OMG, we hate this stuff. You'll find out why real quick. It sends all kinds of fake signals and makes you do a lot more wasted digging than just about anything else, and there is literally TONS of it in the ground. You can notch it out on most machines, but then you'll never find any gold, because gold rings up in the same signal spectrum. This fact is one of the biggest bummers about metal detecting, but you'll get used to it.

Gold – Raw bars of gold bullion, coins, jewelry or anything else made of solid gold of any karat weight; anything else is referred to as "plated."

Gridding Off – Dividing a large hunt area into smaller, more manageable sections to form a grid over the entire area. If casually hunting, you may choose to grid off an area in your imagination only, or use temporary items like sticks or stones, just to make the area less overwhelming. For formal, official archaeological digs, strings are attached to stakes or posts of some sort, set into the ground at measured intervals. Finds are marked with small flags and recorded as both GPS coordinates and measured at depth.

Hole – The access void you dig in the ground to recover a target. Don't leave it a hole when you're done—fill it in!

"Hunted Out" – The notion that everything worth pulling from a certain spot has been found. It's a fallacy: Even if you think everything has been found, there's always something that has eluded everyone before. In areas where the ground freezes, the freeze/thaw/heave cycle churns new stuff toward the surface every year. Therefore, although of course targets become more rare as a spot gets hunted over and over, no place is really ever hunted out.

Hunting – The act of metal detecting; also referred to as MDing, digging, swinging, dirt fishing.

Lesché – (Pronounced leh-SHAY) The brand name for a line of venerable and beloved hand diggers of excellent quality, which look like a garden trowel with one toothed edge. This name is also sometimes used for any model or make of hand digger designed specifically for metal detecting and resembling a genuine Lesché. This use has evolved in the same way that an insulated beverage container is now called a Thermos, whether that's who manufactured it or not.

Jack – The round port into which headphones can be plugged on a metal detector for private sound. Some machines now use wireless headphones and their use in increasing, so at some point, the jack will probably go away. But for now, it's alive and well on all but the most rudimentary detectors.

Key Dates – Coins that are rare for one reason or another.

Large Cent – Any one of a number of designs of U.S. copper one-cent coins minted from 1793-1857. These were roughly an inch in diameter, and were replaced with the smaller, modern penny size in 1858.

Large Coppers – Any of several large copper coins minted during the United States Colonial era and the early 1800s, including half-cent coins minted through 1857. Also referred to as "largies," a term which can also include large cents.

"Merc" – Nickname for silver U.S. dimes minted from 1916-1945, with what appears to be the head of the mythical god Mercury on the front. In actuality, the design was intended by its creator, Adolph Weinman, to be a Winged Liberty Head, but was confused with Mercury and the misidentification stuck. A fasces—a bound bundle of wooden rods, with an axe blade emerging, symbolizing unity and strength—is on the reverse, entwined with an olive branch signifying peace. Like all silver coins, they often emerge from the ground shiny and looking almost new.

"Morgan" – A United States dollar coin minted from 1878 to 1904, and again in 1921; named for its designer, United States Mint Assistant Engraver George T. Morgan. Its obverse depicts a profile portrait of Liberty, while the reverse shows an eagle with outstretched wings.

Nighthawking – The illegal practice of night hunting property for which you don't have permission, in the dark so you're less likely to get caught. This is generally done by unethical people who know they'll never get honest permission, so they go onto other people's property to take what doesn't belong to them. Also called stealing. Nighthawkers tend to also disregard digger etiquette, and often leave ugly, dangerous holes all over the place, making a bad name for the rest of us. Just don't do it. This is not to be confused with legitimate night hunting. There are many reasons people may want to hunt at night on property where they have permission, and this is perfectly legal unless local ordinances forbid it.

On Edge – A coin found standing in a vertical orientation on its edge, rather than lying flat or at an angle underground. This orientation can produce strange signals that even veteran diggers can't always recognize; one reason why digging all signals makes a lot of sense for a newbie.

Peace Dollar – Designed by Anthony de Francisci, this is a United States coin minted from 1921-1928, and again in 1934-1935. The obverse carries a profile of the head and neck of the Goddess of Liberty, with the reverse depicting a resting bald eagle clutching an olive branch, and the legend "Peace" running underneath. This was the last US dollar coin to be struck for circulation in silver.

Pinpointing – Using your metal detector to narrow down your search area by passing it in one direction over the target until figuring out where the signal is strongest, then turning 90° and doing the same thing in the opposite direction. Where both signals are strongest—where they cross—is where the target is located. This can be performed with or without activating the actual pinpointing feature on your detector, though it's usually easier to use it. Pinpointing is also the act of using your handheld pinpointer down inside a recovery hole.

Plug – The generally round clod of dirt and grass you dig to open a hole above your target, which allows you to remove that target from the ground. You start by positioning your digger a few inches to the outside of the target, angling the blade very slightly toward the target, creating slanting walls to the hole. Dig about 4/5 of the way around, but don't complete the circle. Using the part you left uncut as a hinge, use your digger to lever the plug out of the hole and flop it over onto the ground next to it. This way, when you're done digging, it will be very easy to simply push any loose dirt and stones back in the hole and flop the plug back into it, like a stopper in a bottle. It's neat, it's easy, and it's very effective in leaving your hole nearly invisible.

Make sure you step on it to push it back into place before moving on. If the ground is too dry for your plug to hold together, you probably shouldn't dig in that ground anymore until it rains, because the grass on top of the plug will probably die from dehydration, and that will cause problems for the property owner.

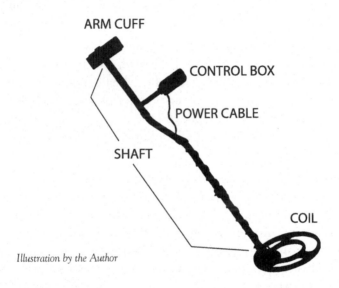

Illustration by the Author

Power Cable – The thick cable, usually black, that runs from your machine's coil to the control box, connecting the metal sensor with the circuitry that creates the signal. Some machines, like the French XP Deus, are now being made using Bluetooth technology instead of analog cables, allowing the digital controls to be contained in a small, relatively flat housing about the size of a smartphone that can be worn on a belt or in a pocket instead of mounted permanently on the shaft.

Pulltabs – The metal "pop-top" rings used to open aluminum beverage cans, and the most annoying thing about metal detecting, because they garbage up an area with big signals for undesirable targets. First introduced to beer cans in 1956, the initial design was a large, round ring attached to an elongated spoon-shaped tab that curled while opening. Nicknamed "beavertails" for their distinctive shape, they were replaced 20 years later by the current, more compact "Sta-Tabs."

These were so named because they are intended to remain attached to the cans to reduce litter and foot lacerations, among other problems. But of course, people are people and have to mess with everything, so you'll find plenty of these later models floating around on and in the ground by themselves.

Repeatable – This is a requirement of a signal that's worth digging. Most soil will produce stray signals all over the place, though you can eliminate many of these by taking the time to properly ground balance and set your sensitivity. But you'll always get a few stray signals, no matter where you hunt. The good signals that indicate an actual target underground are repeatable; that is, you can swing over them again and again and hear the same or a very similar signal every time. The ones you can only hear once or erratically usually indicate soil anomalies and not actual targets.

Relics – Anything you find that has historic interest. It doesn't have to be valuable, it just has to hold historic interest. Also known as "artifacts."

"Seated" – Shorthand for any of the United States silver coins of several denominations bearing a design of a Seated Liberty on the front or obverse face. Minted from the 1830s until the late 1800s. Designed by Christian Gobrecht, U.S Mint Chief Engraver.

Shaft – The tubular frame of the metal detector that holds it all together. Usually it is adjustable for length, using metal pushbutton and/or threaded poly locking mechanisms to hold it in place.

Signal – The audible and/or visual indication your detector produces when your coil passes over a metal object.

Silver – Anything made of sterling or coin silver, or the bars of silver bullion itself

"Skunked" – Having gone metal detecting and returned without finding anything desirable: "Boy, we really got skunked this trip." Alternately, being outdone by a hunting partner with a really good discovery, when all you found was something lame. Which, when you're starting, is almost nothing: Everything you find is cool when you're first learning to hunt, so enjoy it!

"Standing" – Nickname for the silver U.S. Standing Liberty Quarter, designed by Hermon Atkins MacNeil, minted 1916-1930.

Swinging – The act of using your metal detector, since most machines require side-to-side movement to operate properly. You can always tell someone who's never used a machine before: They hold it in one place and wait for a beep.

Target – Any metal object that causes your detector to give off a signal; the thing you're hunting for.

"Toasted" – The condition of a coin that's been in the ground so long that most or all surface designs and markings are obscured by oxidation, encrustation or are just plain worn off; unable to be read with any clarity.

Trash – Any unwanted item you may encounter underground while you're hunting (areas with lots of, say, foil or pulltabs or bottle caps strewn about or with lots of iron farther underground is considered "trashy"). Trash can also take the form of targets you dug but do not value. Digger etiquette requires that you pack out all trash you find in or on top of the ground, so I recommend carrying a trash bag with you in your vehicle, in which to dump your unwanted finds.

Treasure Hunting – Seeking items of value (though they may only hold value for you), using a metal detector or not. Some people hunt for treasure in the form of arrowheads or points; gemstones or pretty rocks; old bottles; the list in infinite. Also called "TH-ing." Metal detecting is just one kind of treasure hunting.

"Walker" – Nickname for the U.S. Walking Liberty half-dollar, designed by Adolph Weinman and minted in coin silver from 1916-1947.

"Wheat Penny" – Copper U.S. pennies with two wheat shafts that form a wreath-like frame on the back or reverse face of the coin. Produced between 1909 and 1956, these coins are made of copper and generally hold up well in the soil. Also called "wheats" or "wheaties."

"Zincoln" – Derogatory nickname for U.S. pennies with the Lincoln Memorial on reverse face, made mostly of zinc with a thin copper coating. These coins are deceptively light in weight, and do not last long in the ground. The copper coating provides almost no protection for the main zinc body, which corrodes really quickly in the ground. These are frequently in very bad shape when found, looking like someone has chewed them around the edges, even if they haven't been in the soil very long. Those dropped in farm fields and lawns, where chemically based fertilizers are used, deteriorate the fastest.

The Hobby

Metal detecting has a few rules, some more general and others more specific. When you're just starting, it's easier to follow them. Later on, you'll figure out what's comfortable for you. This section also contains some general observations and suggestions.

1. **Read your detector's user manual** and/or watch the instruction video. Seriously, of any other tip I can give you in this book, this one's the most important. Because each machine is different and has its own operating idiosyncrasies, it is probably the easiest, most important and most direct step you can take to ensure that your initial detecting sessions are fruitful and enjoyable. The user information provided with your machine thoroughly explains its features and functions, different signal tones, and how it behaves under varying conditions. Yet, I'm amazed how many people have never read their operator's manual or even watched the "Getting Started" DVD that comes with nearly all modern detectors. I did read and watch mine—more than once—and keep them around in case I need to refer back in the future for some particular reason, and I believe I'm a better treasure hunter for it. You will do yourself a huge favor by reading through your manual and/or watching your provided video at least once before you get started, because I guarantee that if you don't, you'll wind up being very frustrated to the point where you'll eventually read or watch them anyway. Save yourself the irritation and just read or watch them first.

2. **Practice, practice, practice.** I cannot stress this highly enough. It's like any other skill: You only get better by actually doing it, especially when it comes to learning

the idiosyncrasies of your particular machine. You can read as much as you want about metal detecting, and you can watch thousands of videos of other people doing it, and I recommend doing both. But the only way you will build your own skill as a detectorist and your knowledge about potential targets is to get out there and detect and dig!

3. **Patience, patience, patience.** This is the third-most-important concept to remember about metal detecting. There's a lot to learn about your machine, accessories and potential targets. It's not difficult, but it does take time to learn, so you will not "get" everything right away. To avoid disappointment, adjust your expectations accordingly, and be kind to yourself in learning this hobby.

   Expect to spend a significant amount of time getting to know your machine, and by this I mean getting out in the field and working with it. This is definitely a "learning by doing" pursuit. I had a very low-end machine when I first started, and wasn't able to get out to practice hunting very often. Consequently, it was at least three months after I started swinging my first detector that I found anything other than square nails and junk, and a good year before I found my first modern coin. But those little victories were enough of a thrill to keep me going for two more years, until I could upgrade my machine. And it wasn't until I got my third machine in my seventh year of digging that I finally felt I knew a bit about what I was doing. I don't think I'll ever feel like a "veteran," but I learn something new every time I go out.

4. **Always remain a student.** It's easy after you've been digging for a while to think you know all there is to know about detecting and about the things you might find. Here's a secret: You never will, so don't expect to.

You can't help but learn more every time you go hunting, especially if you go with other people willing to share their knowledge. You will benefit most if you share what you know when asked, and admit when you don't know something. Don't be too proud to ask for help, and don't be a blowhard about what you do know. The most experienced and knowledgeable people I know in this hobby are the quietest and most humble. Beware the ones always boasting about their knowledge and trying to impress. That kind of behavior is usually born of insecurity.

5. **Actively seek the knowledge of detecting veterans.** There are tons of places to find veteran detectorists you can learn from. I list some of them in the Resources section of this book. And if you're lucky enough to hunt with experienced detectorists, keep your eyes and ears open, and your mouth shut (other than to ask brief questions). Being given the opportunity to learn from veteran diggers who really know their stuff (and when you're a newbie, nearly everyone knows more than you do) is a true gift. Treat it that way. Be appreciative and show your gratitude for what they share with you.

6. **Beware of poseurs and trolls.** Unfortunately, as in any endeavor that takes a certain amount of skill to master, metal detecting has its share of phonies and negative people. If you go to any of the places metal detectorists hang out online, you will undoubtedly run into your share of both, and it won't take long.

   There are people who will copy photos of someone else's finds from eBay or some other site and post them as their own. There are those who will talk constantly about everything they've found and who seem to have an abundance of advice for others, but who—strangely, for someone who seems so completely into the hobby—never seem to show up anywhere in person, or if they do, never seem to actually find much. Then there are the nasties, who seem to derive pleasure only from denigrating other diggers. They may spread ugly rumors online about other detectorists for no apparent reason, or always have to be Debbie Downer by downplaying others' luck and skill or otherwise casting aspersions when someone else is sharing a cool find.

Who knows why these people act this way? Perhaps they're insecure about their own skills, or are jealous of someone else's detector or finds. Or maybe they're just unpleasant people. Whatever the reason, it's best to simply ignore these trolls. They thrive on attention of any sort, and will generally go away if it is denied by those of us who refuse to encourage their bad behavior by engaging them. Certainly don't allow them to ruin your fun for any reason.

What Kind of Hunter Are You?

There are many ways to enjoy the hobby of metal detecting. You don't need to choose any one particular specialization, but it's helpful to be aware of the many different ways in which people come into the hobby, and how they sometimes choose to focus their efforts in narrower areas of interest.

It's best to begin as a generalist to expose yourself to all the options available. As you get more experienced, you may find yourself interested in choosing any one or a combination of specializations, as you develop your own interests.

Most folks remain generalists, and there are few diggers who are strict in their preference for a certain kind of machine, target or location; others are happy just to get out hunting, regardless where it is—few serious treasure hunters can turn down any opportunity to dig a little history, whatever it may be.

Besides, despite what you may know about the history of any given dig spot, there could be anything there. That mystery is half the fun!

7. **Beach** – Beach hunters generally work beach areas immediately after the close of public bathing hours. They may first search the dry sand where beach towels and blankets were spread, in hopes of finding dropped jewelry, keys, coins, toys and other valuables. They also use water-resistant detectors to scan the surf zone, to find items that may have been washed out of pockets and bathing suits. They may even venture a bit farther out to the first breaker line, to find items that have been washed toward the shore from deeper water, including coins and relics from sunken ships just off the coast in some areas. It's important to note that beach hunters must use a

detector that will operate without static or interference in or near saltwater.

Without going into all the details, the two main types of machines are Very Low Frequency (VLF), which are the most common; and Pulse Induction (PI), which are more specialized. Both read signals in different ways, and the best one for the beach is a PI machine that doesn't react to salts in the sand or water. You can use certain VLF machines with serious ground balancing and sensitivity controls, but those aren't usually in the budget of most beginners. So if you're going to mostly hunt beaches, you really want a PI detector.

8. **Buttons and Buckles** – Many detectorists find their interests leaning toward the many different types and styles of buttons from across the eras. Buttons of all shapes, sizes, designs and manufacture, were originally used as closures on all manner of clothing and accessories. The same goes for buckles, from hand-forged iron to brass, steel and tin; from the much sought after shoe and knee buckles of the Colonial era through the coveted belt and strap buckle plates of the Civil War and on through modern times.

9. **Cellar Hole Specialist** – These detectorists prefer to research and find foundation cavities or "cellar holes" left over from long-gone buildings such as homesteads, barns, sheds, taverns and stores. They enjoy the challenge of locating these hot spots, where they often find all kinds of relics and coins left by former inhabitants.

10. **Coinshooter** – This is the term given to those who find particular fascination with the coins (and sometimes tokens) unearthed in their hunts. It is probably the most common area of specialization

among detectorists. Coinshooters often turn into numismatists (coin collectors and enthusiasts) through learning about the coins they find.

11. **Deepwater** – Deepwater detectorists may hunt on the ocean floor or at the bottom of freshwater lakes. This generally takes some training as a scuba diver, although some hunters do free dive, using snorkels. Again, deepwater ocean divers must use a machine that doesn't react erratically to saltwater. Both saltwater and freshwater deep divers must use a detector rated for significant depth. Lower-end water-resistant detectors are generally rated for safe operation only at 10 feet or less; deeper than that, and their seals may fail, ruining the machine. So if you're going to deepwater hunt, make sure to buy a machine rated for such depths.

12. **Field and/or Forest** – Some diggers prefer to specialize according to a favorite type of location, rather than according to any particular type of target. Some folks like the relative ease of finding and swinging over open fields. Others prefer the more strenuous slogging through underbrush and a usually higher concentration of biting and stinging insects in the woods. Why? Because these conditions tend to keep such areas from being as heavily hunted, and so can yield more and better items. The forest can also hide cellar holes, old walls and forgotten roads whose booty is just waiting to be discovered by those willing to work a bit harder for their rewards. Winter is a good time to dig in the forest, because most underbrush is wilted back and leaf litter keeps the ground from freezing in all but the most brutal cold. It's also helpful that insects and most other critters that could be a nuisance or danger are in hibernation.

13. **Generalist** – This is how we all start, from the thrill of first finding something—anything—at all. Most of us remain in this category, happy to dig whatever might pass beneath our coils. But as we become more experienced, some of us discover a growing preference for one or several particular kinds of prize, and just naturally gravitate to that specialization.

14. **Seasonal or Year-Round** – As humans who enjoy physical comfort, most detectorists are seasonal treasure hunters, at least in the northern climes of the Lower 48. In the sunny south, the weather is generally amenable to metal detecting year-round, as far as comfortable temperatures go. In the north, however, winter's cold temperatures can freeze the ground solid, making it as difficult to dig as concrete. Targets there may lie beneath several inches or even feet of snow in addition to the usual soil overburden, and extreme cold may make the hunter's hands and feet uncomfortable to the point of loss of feeling and fine motor control, so most northern diggers hang up their equipment after the first snowfall and don't go out hunting again until spring thaw.

    But there are many diehards who will go out in all types of weather and temperatures, especially if they have woods nearby, because a heavy layer of snow—especially on top of a layer of leaves—can serve as insulation to keep the ground from freezing. If you do plan to be an all-season hunter, it's a good idea to invest in a water-resistant machine, and to remember that long exposure to extreme cold can damage some more sensitive machines. Also, dress accordingly in layers that can be added or removed as needed.

15. **War Relics** – If you haven't guessed from the rest of these descriptions, detectorists tend to become avid

collectors of certain items they find and take a fancy to. This tends to make them specialize in hunting those particular items, and nowhere is this truer than with those who like to find relics of battles and wars and the time periods in which they were fought. Not always, but often, these diggers will specialize in a certain conflict, and sometimes even in particular periods or locations of that conflict.

In America, this includes everything from frontier skirmishes during early settlement, to battles during the heyday of the beaver fur trade, the French & Indian War, the Revolutionary War, the War of 1812, the Spanish-American War, the American Civil War, the Indian Wars, and all the foreign wars in which our country has engaged.

16. **Water (Rivers, Lakes & Streams)** – This is a category separate from beach hunting, because it's generally a freshwater activity that doesn't require a special saltwater-ready machine. It's usually best to use a fully submersible (waterproof) machine for deeper streams and rivers, as it's very easy to lose your footing on slippery rocks and drop your machine in the water. However, if you're in knee-deep or shallower water, most machines can be safely submersed in water up to the control box, which must be kept dry. It's a good idea to use some kind of "leash"—a cord or cable—attached to your detector at one end and to your person at the other, to keep from having it float downstream if you fall or while you're digging or diving to retrieve a target.

Related Specialties

17. **Privy Digging** – Many people get into metal detecting through the hobby of "privy digging." Privy is another word for outhouse. Outhouses used to

do double duty as both latrine and general trash pit. People threw lots of trash they couldn't burn down those holes, including ceramic, glass and metal items. Privies were also favorite stashing areas in which to get rid of incriminating evidence of most kinds.

These days, many of those objects are much sought after as antiques and collectibles. Since the smelly, disgusting human waste has long since dried up and turned to inoffensive soil, there is no shortage of people willing to dig up those old holes to see what treasures they can unearth.

People have found everything from full bottles of whiskey and hunting knives to loaded guns (NOTE: If you find a real gun, most states require that you immediately report it and turn it in to your local police, in case it was involved in a crime) and beautiful ceramic treasures in privy digs. Metal detectorists may become privy diggers through friends who hunt their treasures this way, as well.

18. **Arrowheads** – Of course, arrowheads are made of stone and can't be found with a metal detector. But detectorists often hunt recently plowed farm fields to see what the plow blade has churned up, and will come across arrowheads and other points in the process. Some diggers take an interest in finding and collecting these non-metal artifacts, as well.

19. **Bottles** – Along with privy digging, another large source of old bottles is what are called "bottle dumps." These large deposits of old, empty bottles are frequently found out in the country near places that used to be taverns, restaurants and general stores, where for a long time there was no public sanitation or trash pickup. Private residents used to toss bottles out the back door or down over an embankment, along with other trash. People now

hunt through them for desirable collectibles, some of which are truly beautiful, rare, valuable, or all three.

Many detectorists hunting old basements, walls and crawlspaces often come across old bottles. You may even find them out in the middle of a field or forest, and once you dig up your first cool old bottle, it's hard not to get hooked into collecting them. They can embody a great deal of history and the many different ways they were manufactured are fascinating.

20. **Many Others** – These are but a few of the more common relic/artifact specializations. There are many more, and chances are if you can collect it, someone out there specializes in it. Most of us must limit our collecting instincts to what will fit in the amount of space we have in our homes and storage areas to keep and maybe display our finds. Others are limited to the types of items to be found near their homes. These limitations don't seem to pose much problem for a motivated digger.

Equipment

You don't need to go broke buying equipment. You may have heard that metal detecting equipment is expensive, and it can be. But a beginner can get started for under $100. It's generally true that you get what you pay for in terms of performance and durability, in your detector and all accessories. But there are a few low-cost alternatives that will get the job done, and if you're just starting out and aren't sure if you'll stick with the hobby or not, it's generally best to start small and upgrade as needed.

Must-haves

There are a few pieces of equipment you must have if you're going to be at all successsful as a metal detectorist. There are also items that are nice to have, but aren't necessary. We cover these in this section and the next.

Metal Detector

Of course, the first and most important piece of equipment is your detector itself. It's not my aim to endorse any particular brand or model of detector, but I will share my personal experience with actual machines where applicable. Mentions of any and all makes and models in this book are based solely on my personal experience actually using those machines, or on machines I have seen in operation firsthand. This certainly does not reflect in any way on those machines I don't mention: It simply reflects the extent of my personal experience.

22. **Buy the best detector you can afford,** but don't go overboard. There are models that don't do much more than beep when they pass over something very close to the surface, and others that will not only tell you a target is present, but also how deep it is, what type of metal it's made of, if it's down there alone or

in the company of other metal objects, how big it is, and even its general shape. Some really high-end models have ground-penetrating radar (GPR) and can give you a digital image of your target!

As you might imagine, the ones that have fewer functions are generally more affordable, and the ones with lots of bells and whistles can run into the tens of thousands of dollars, especially if they're all tricked out with add-ons and accessories. But here's the secret: Until you know how to operate any machine, you can't even understand the bells and whistles, much less make good use of them. Again: buy a good, basic machine and learn everything you can about it. In a contest, I'd put my money on a veteran digger with a very basic machine who has practiced a long time with it, than a newbie detectorist using a fancy new machine he has no experience with.

23. **Basic Features** – Truly rudimentary machines pretty much just turn on and off and make a noise when their coils pass over something metal. My first one was like that, and I honestly wouldn't recommend these unless you're either just fooling around or only want to find, say, property markers or something like that. You will quickly become frustrated and disenchanted, and since there are better machines to be had for about the same money, it just doesn't make sense to buy one that will only make you mad. There are many, many features available on the diverse array of machines, but there's a set of about eight that are really necessary or at least extremely nice to have. The same feature can vary a bit from one metal detector to another, but they're all pretty similar. A good basic options/features set includes:

• *Discrimination* – Lets your machine ignore or "notch out" those types of metal you're not interested in digging. I have yet to meet a machine whose discrimination is perfect, so for several reasons (and they won't always be the same, because environmental conditions may vary), you'll always get some of what you don't want; but this feature really helps keep it to a minimum.

- *Target ID* – Just what it sounds like, this feature gives you a pretty good idea of what's under your coil. I say "pretty good," because again, this is never a foolproof function. Ground conditions, depth and the proximity of other metal objects can pull one over on even the best of machines. But target identification is, in my experience, more often right than wrong, and I have noticed that some detectors do a better job of this than others.

- *Tone ID* – It's very helpful to have at least two or three differently pitched tones that will sound according to what type of metal you're over. For instance, my first detector had just one tone, so I ended up digging everything. Though I did end up with a few good finds this way, I also dug an amazing amount of junk and this was very tiring. A two-tone machine like my second detector was great: the low, "grunting" sound always meant iron, and a high tone meant something good. If the tone sounded multiple times quite close together in a way that very much resembled the clanging of a slot machine that has just hit the jackpot, I knew it was something really good. I now have a multiple-tone machine and though it will produce up to nine different sounds, I find that kind of overkill. I can't easily memorize nine, but a low grunt for iron, medium tone for non-ferrous and a high tone for silver and copper is plenty for me. Your mileage may vary.

- *Depth Indicator* – Especially for the beginner, this really is mandatory. If you've been digging a while, you may develop the ability to get a good sense of how far down a target is by the strength of the tone, but this is a real skill and not everyone develops it. So, having a depth indicator on your machine is extremely helpful. Be aware that depths shown on your indicator are approximate. Some manufacturers will cop to this reality, some not, but I have yet to see a truly accurate depth indicator.

- *Sensitivity* – You really want to be able to adjust how sensitive your machine is reading the ground, because if you're in a heavily mineralized area, or you have electrical interference such as an underground dog fence, buried or overhead power cables nearby, your machine may start to chatter like a lonely person who hasn't seen another human being in years. It's very distracting, and being able to turn down your sensitivity to avoid it can mean the difference between a pleasant, productive hunt and an annoying bust.

- *Multiple modes or programs* – This feature is only available on digital machines, and means the detector comes with pre-set "programs" that have certain metals or objects "notched out," allowing you to concentrate on one kind or another. Even some beginner machines now offer this feature, and it's really nice to have.

- *Power/Low battery indicator* – This just seems like a complete no-brainer to me. You don't want to be surprised in the middle of a field, a long way from your vehicle (where I hope you are carrying at least one extra set of batteries), by a machine that just goes dead without warning. However, very basic machines don't offer this feature, and I'd just bypass those.

- *Pinpointing* – Having a pinpointing feature built into your detector is one of the most helpful things you'll have in the field. Some diggers view this as a luxury, but I don't. It's generally activated by a button of some sort, and allows you to really zero in on your target by listening to the more sensitive tones than you get while just swinging without activating the onboard pinpoint feature. My first machine didn't have this, and the holes I dug were as large as trash can lids because I was unpracticed and didn't know what to look or listen for. You can do a rudimentary type of pseudo-pinpointing by repeatedly running your coil over a spot until you find the loudest, strongest, most steady signal, then turning 90° to the way you were swinging and repeating that maneuver. Where the two loudest/most stable tones cross is where your target is. But with a real pinpointing feature, it's a hundred times easier and takes far less time.

- *Headphone jack* – I have seen detectors without this feature, but they have all been older models. These days, I think this may be pretty much a given. Not only is the ability to use headphones nice, so you can hear the softer tones of deeply buried small objects like coins, but it's also the polite thing to do when you're hunting with other diggers or just want to avoid being obnoxious to anyone else who may pass by. We detectorists love that beeping sound, but to others it can be truly annoying. You don't want to annoy someone who has allowed you to hunt their property!

24. Additional, really helpful but not absolutely necessary detector features include:

- *Volume control* – I know you can live without this one, because I did for three years when I first started detecting…but BOY, was I glad to be able to turn the volume down, especially when I wore headphones! Without it, sound can be painful.

- *Ground Balancing* – This feature allows you to compensate for mineralized soil, essentially rendering the ground invisible to the detector so it won't interfere with it reading a target's signal. Most machines do offer ground balancing now, and some do it automatically for you. To be honest, I have effectively hunted without it most of my time in the hobby because at first I just didn't really understand what ground balancing does. I understand it now, but frankly think sometimes this feature seems more of a wish than a reality.

  Most machines I've used require you to do some kind of pumping up and down while depressing the pinpointer button until you don't hear any tone, but I have tried this for years and years and still have never gotten the machine to go silent. One of my detectors now has auto ground balancing, so I just turn it on and start hunting. I believe most hunters think this is a must-have, but clearly it's not, because even all those years I didn't "get it," I still found lots of good stuff.

  Perhaps I just have a higher threshold of annoyance for chatter and false signals. Or maybe the machines eventually adjusted to the ground as I hunted—a sort of pseudo-ground tracking—and my success was a result of that.

- *Ground Tracking* – Think of this as continuous, automatic ground balancing. If you're hunting a patch of ground that's pretty consistent, you'll likely only need to ground balance once as you start hunting. But if you're on a large plot of ground that changes over some distance or when you encounter natural features such as waterways, swales, rocky ledges and outcroppings, etc., you may find you need to re-balance every so often. This can be a pain, so ground tracking is a nice feature to have, because it will automatically take care of that for you.

- *Backlit screen* – Another thing you can definitely live without, but once you have it, you won't want to be without it. This feature lets you hunt even after the sun has gone down, and is also helpful in deeply shaded areas such as in the woods or on the shadow side of a building or land feature.

- *Waterproof/submersible* – Unless you're specifically intending to hunt in the surf on beaches or in deeper rivers and creeks, this is one feature you really can live without, maybe forever. After all, you can submerge the coil and shaft on most detectors with no harm done, as long as you keep the control box dry. But once you start wanting to hunt streams or rivers more than knee-deep or with any kind of current, or beach surf areas, you won't want to risk an accidental spill. Waterway environments are very slippery and surf is, by definition, rough and can easily knock you over, so you're tempting fate by entering them with a machine that you can't get fully underwater without damaging it. There are a few levels of submersibility, starting with about 10 feet of depth and going deeper from there. Generally, the deeper it goes, the more it costs.

Accessories

Aside from your detector itself, there are accessories you'll want to seriously consider.

25. **Pinpointer** – Here, I'm referring to the handheld type of pinpointer. These are generally about the size of a flashlight, and most are self-contained though there are a few detectors that have a detachable one on a cable. Pinpointers are extremely helpful for fitting into the hole after you've dug it (since most holes are too small for the coil itself to fit in), so you can locate the exact position of your target. I honestly consider this accessory "must-have" equipment now, because finally buying a handheld pinpointer was such a significant game-changer in the ease and success of my hunts, I would no longer even consider hunting without one. I have literally turned around and headed home when realizing I've forgotten my pinpointer, because for me it's no longer fun to hunt without one, just frustrating.

    It's not the cheapest tool—decent ones run between about $80-175—but without one, your holes will be enormous and you'll spend a frustrating amount of time locating your target in the hole. Sometimes it's still challenging to locate a tiny item even with one! I have used and like the original Garrett ProPointer (black, non-submersible), the Garrett AT ProPointer (orange – also called the "Garrett Carrot" – and submersible), and the DeteKnix Xpointer (various colors, not submersible). I have to say that the reason I got the latter was because my original Garrett got to the point after several years of use where it falsed a great deal, which just won't work with a pinpointer. The orange version does not have this problem. I have friends who've "doctored" their black ones so they won't false, but in my mind, if you're going to spend that much money on a piece of equipment, you shouldn't have to do that. A couple of my dig buddies have the White's TRX Bullseye waterproof pinpointers, and really love them. You can buy a handheld "metal detector" at Harbor Freight Tools for about $20, which is essentially a long stud finder, and it will be better than no pinpointer at all. But you definitely get what you pay for when it comes to these, so invest wisely.

26. **Hand Digger** – Next to your detector and pinpointer, your digging tool is most critical to being able to quickly and easily recover a target, so its quality and comfort really matter. There are different kinds of digging tools for different types of work, but here I'm talking about a small, hand-held, trowel-like shovel. In fact, I started with a simple gardening trowel from the dollar store. Since I wasn't able to get out hunting much in my first three years, it lasted that whole time. But once I moved up to a better detector and got a pinpointer, I was finding a lot more targets and doing a lot more digging, and the trowel soon bit the dust. I bent it trying to pry rocks out of the ground, then promptly snapped it off at the handle. It had served its purpose well, but it was time to move up to something more substantial.

    I asked for a Lesche-type digger made of military grade steel, that also had teeth tooled into one side of the blade for sawing through roots. I still use that tool today and imagine I will for the rest of my hunting career. These days, there are a few digging tools that, quality-wise, fall in between the dollar store trowel and the $60 professional digger.

    The one I like best is the garden scoop from Fiskars. They cost about $8.00, and you can find them in gardening centers, big box home centers and at some discount chain stores. They're cast from a single piece of metal with a plastic handle, so they're pretty durable. I keep one as a backup or to lend to friends on a hunt. I do not recommend using the composite carbon-plastic diggers unless your area has very soft, sandy soil, because you just can't get the leverage you sometimes need with heavier clay soils and big rocks, such as we have in my area.

27. **Finds Pouch** – Most major detector manufacturers offer some kind of zip pouch on a webbing belt, in which to put your finds. I use one of those now, since one came with my last detector, but for ten years I simply used a carpenter's nail apron, and was perfectly happy with that. I especially liked the one I had that had a leather hammer loop on either side, providing a perfect place to carry my pinpointer. The good thing for beginners is that generally you can find nail aprons very cheap at flea markets, thrift stores or even free during special promotional days at your favorite hardware store, and most of them have at least two pockets – one for your keepers and one for your trash finds. The only place a nail apron won't work is in the water. There, you need a pouch that zips shut so your finds won't get washed out, and which is made of netting rather than solid material, so the water can pass through instead of filling up the pouch and slowing you down.

28. **Batteries** – It seems silly to even list this, but I can't tell you how many of my own hunts have been cut short because my batteries died in my detector or pinpointer, and I didn't have any extras with me. I always put batteries on my Christmas list so I know I'll have enough every year, and I keep at least one fresh change of batteries with me for any gear that uses that uses them. TIP: If your detector batteries

are at half charge or less, don't just keep new ones in your vehicle, bring them with you on your hunt. They're not that heavy, and there's nothing more annoying than being quite a ways from your car when your batteries conk out. If it happens late enough in the day, it can effectively end your hunt if you're too tired to make that trek and back again.

29. **Comfortable, protective footwear** – What type is a matter of personal preference, but take it seriously. I've seen diggers wear everything but slippers into the field, but there does seem to be a preference for hunting or hiking boots. This makes good sense, since they're built rugged, have a thick sole for protection and comfort, and substantial, protective uppers to avoid scratches from sticks, brambles and manmade hazards such as broken glass and barbed wire. For this reason, sandals and flip-flops are not a good choice for digging footwear, unless you're on the beach (and even then, I'd recommend surf mocs of some kind).

    I prefer a substantial pair of athletic walking shoes when I'll be in residential lawn areas or in the water. I've used surf mocs, but they don't really protect from rocky bottoms as much as I'd like, especially in rivers with a stronger current. In rough fields or wooded areas, a pair of medium-height, nylon upper hiking boots are protective but not too heavy. You have to think about this to avoid fatigue setting in too early. When I was first starting and went into the field, I kept a pair of gel inserts when I knew I'd be walking more than a few hours, but discovered I didn't really need them. If you have lace-up boots, keep a spare pair of laces in your gear bag. You need to be able to depend on your shoes so they don't distract you from the hunt.

30. **Comfortable clothing** – Wear clothes that allow free movement but still cover your arms and legs to protect from bugs, burrs, brambles and poison ivy. It's advisable to wear long pants if you hunt in areas where ticks are prevalent, and to keep the cuffs tight around your ankles, because those little buggers will crawl right up a loose pant leg. (And remember to check yourself for ticks as thoroughly as possible before getting in your vehicle to go home: You don't want to bring any unwelcome hitchhikers home!) If you're reactive to poison ivy, oak or sumac, it's a good idea to carry some IvyX poison block and apply it to all exposed skin before going out in the field. The best way to dress in ideal hunting weather—spring and fall, when there are few temperature extremes—is in layers. This way you can bulk up or peel off as needed.

Nice-To-Haves

31. **Long-Handled Digger** – If you don't like to have to drop to your knees for exploratory holes, or you just appreciate the better leverage you can get with a long-handled digger, I recommend getting one. I began with essentially a half-size spade with a D-handle that's light and easy to carry. You may also use a specialty spade such as a folding camp shovel (known in the military as an entrenching tool), but I find the latter a bit too prone to snapping under heavy leverage, which you will encounter now and then. About three years ago, a kind fellow digger gave me his 31-inch tubular steel shaft Lesche Samson T-handle Shovel—intended for detectorists—when he upgraded, and I've been using that happily ever since. I must admit that since trying out a Piranha long-handled digger from Predator Tools, I've been saving up to get one. The

more angled blade shape and the rubber footpads on the back help it cut through even thickly rooted turf like a hot knife through butter.

32. **Headphones** – I don't consider these "must have" equipment, but they really are nice to have when you need them. I hunted without headphones for years, but after a while discovered that sometimes, I'd really like to shut out the ambient noise so I can hear faint signals, which can indicate deep coins that tend to be older and more valuable. This is especially true when hunting close to a roadway with lots of passing traffic. I even came to use them in my front yard, which was on a major roadway that had significant loud motor-cycle traffic on the same nice days I wanted to be out hunting. Remember that if you're hunting with a submersible machine in a water environment, you need to have waterproof headphones, too.

33. **Control Box Cover** – Unless you're running a waterproof or water-resistant machine, most of your detector can get wet except the control box. So if you think it may rain on your hunt, it's a good idea to pop for a weatherproof cover for your control box, custom made by the manufacturer to fit your machine, about $10-12 each. Or you can use the low-cost alternative: a zipper-lock plastic sandwich bag. The latter aren't the best-fitting, but they are effective for the most part, and they're disposable, so when they get worn, you can cheaply and easily replace them.

   You may want to keep a box of these bags with your gear anyway, since they often come in handy for storing small finds so they don't scatter all over the place before you get home, if you don't want to leave them in your finds pouch for some reason. They also help keep used batteries together until you can properly dispose of them, and could serve a number of other purposes.

34. **Probe** – Some detectorists, especially those with some years of experience under their belts, like to use a long probe to stick into the ground before digging. These probes are made of a softer metal such as brass, and when pushed slowly into the ground, will hit your target and tell you how deep it is, without scratching harder metals such as those used to make coins. This is a good way to make sure you don't accidentally hit and ding your target, since that can seriously devalue a coin or relic. These tools look like screwdrivers. I have one but never got good enough with it to make it worthwhile to carry. I just tend to dig a wider plug than most, and I've only hit one or two things that way in a dozen years of digging.

35. **Headlamp** – If you live in an area where daytime hunting is just too hot and you like to hunt at night, or you frequently hunt in crawlspaces, basements and other dark places, you may find a headlamp a worthwhile investment. I have four, which I buy when I see them on sale at hardware stores for $5.00 or less. I've used them once or twice when the hunt was too good to stop but the sun was going down. Why so many? I try to keep at least one backup of every piece of equipment I might need in case something breaks in the field, and also lend them out to fellow diggers who may need them. Generally, I don't night hunt because I live in the country where there are skunks, rabid raccoons, coyotes, black bears and even wildcats that come out at night, so I don't often use a headlamp and can't make recommendations on best models, features or prices for those who might use one a lot.

36. **Cell or smartphone** – Now, I have this listed under "nice to have," because you don't technically need this to metal detect. But quite honestly, I consider a cell or smartphone part of my safety gear, especially since I often hunt alone. It just makes good sense. I also use the camera on my smartphone to take photos or videos of my digs, and sometimes to text particularly interesting shots to some of my best digging buddies, to share the joy of a special find.

    I also sometimes use it to make notes about my finds or locations. There are even smartphone apps created specifically for metal detectorists, for logging hunts, finds and GPS information. If you are going to bring your expensive phone into the field with you, I strongly recommend investing in an Otterbox or similarly heavy duty protective case to keep the dirt and moisture out of it. At the very least, use a screen protector to avoid scratches and some kind of enclosure case. It's also not a bad idea to check your phone's jacks and ports for stray crumbs of dirt after a hunt, and blow anything out with compressed air.

37. **Camera** – I use the one on my smartphone to record special digs and finds, but am saving for a GoPro so I can create hands-free videos, too. I've sometimes taken a photo of a spot I want to come back to without leaving any physical markers in the field. I take it from a spot where I can kind of triangulate between existing points of reference, such as a tree, a rock and a fence post, so I have a pretty good idea where I was at.

38. **Water** – Again, this is in the "nice to have" section because if you're only going to be hunting for an hour or so and you've just had something to drink, you don't need to haul a water bottle with

you. But if it's hot or you're going to be afield for a while, I'd consider this a "must have" item. It's critically important to stay well-hydrated in the field, especially when it's hot.

I bought a $5.00 camo pouch at a local military surplus store to hold a water bottle, and I use it every hunt. If I'm going to be out for several hours, I will tuck another bottle into my finds pouch, too. Take your hydration seriously—I've seen more than one digger succumb to heat exhaustion because he didn't drink enough while he was hunting (and beer or coffee don't count—caffeine and alcohol actually contribute to dehydration). It's a bummer of a way to end your hunt, and if it turns into heat stroke, it can be downright dangerous to your longterm health.

39. **Gloves** – This is another of those items that isn't absolutely necessary: I know several detectorists who dig bare-handed. But the one time I did that, after ten years of digging, I of course grabbed onto a rusty coffee can lid, and slit my thumb open. The rest of what should have been a pleasant afternoon hunt was spent in the very expensive, very un-fun emergency room, getting a tetanus shot (which all diggers should stay current on, gloves or no).

Try several different types to protect your hands. Cheaper cotton gloves dipped in rubber work well to keep your hands dry in very damp soil, while more expensive, fitted gloves with friction dots or strips give you better control and sensory information, and their material provides some protection from puncture and cold.

I probably have ten pairs of gloves floating around in my gear bag, and one of them is a pretty decent pair of construction worker gloves I paid about $8.00 for. They're made of substantial synthetic material, insulated and with water-resistent palms and fingers. On a cool day, I appreciate not having my fingers go numb, so they're worth the extra expense.

40. **Knee pads** – If you even think you might have problems kneeling, get a pair of knee pads. I have pretty serious knee problems from an old skiing injury, so I couldn't hunt without them. They don't have to be expensive, but anything less than $10/pair will likely not hold up very long. My first few pairs, usually meant for rollerblading, I bought in the sporting goods department of thrift stores.

    I used standard ones for years, but my later pairs had a hard shell on the outside, which really help when kneeling in rocky soil. I just recently bought my first pair of gel-filled knee pads, and appreciate the added comfort. Some diggers always kneel on the same knee and only use a single knee pad, so a pair lasts them twice as long.

41. **Bandanna** – There are many uses for a bandanna or two in the field. I mostly use mine to pile dirt on when digging a hole in a manicured lawn. This keeps you from having to collect it all from the grass afterward, since you can simply gather the corners together and dump it quickly and easily back into the hole. I have also used a bandanna:

    - as a makeshift sweatband on my forehead, to keep stinging sweat from rolling into my eyes

    - tucked up under my cap and hanging down to cover the back of my neck and protect it from the sun

    - wetted down to hang around my neck and cool me off in the heat of summer

- with its corners tied together, to create a makeshift finds pouch when my real one got too full while I was far from my vehicle

- covered with bug spray and worn on my head to keep the biting flies away

- as a napkin after a field lunch

- to wipe off my glasses (be careful with plastic lenses!), phone screen or detector display when covered by windblown dust

- to clean off my muddy pinpointer

- to temporarily wrap a cut finger

I'm sure you'll be able to find many uses of your own for this cheap, versatile field tool.

42. **Hat or cap** – In warm weather, you should protect your head from the sun, but not everyone does. A ball cap is the most common headgear for this, as the brim helps keep the sun out of your eyes, too, which is a huge help when you're trying to read your detector's display. Wide-brimmed hats like gardeners wear are also a lightweight option. In cooler weather, ski hats, hunting caps or other warm models work well to keep your head warm. Hoodie sweatshirts can be pulled up over your cap if the wind comes up to protect from earaches.

43. **Neck protection** – If you hunt in sunny weather and aren't wearing a coat, it's a good idea to cover your neck in the back to protect from sunburn. Remember, most of the time you're hunting, your head is down and your neck is exposed unless you have long hair. You can tuck a large bandanna under your cap to let it trail down over your neck, or buy a hat with a built-in

neck shade like one of those Foreign Legion kepis. You can also purchase sun shields designed to work with hats from sporting goods stores or suppliers for road crew and construction workers.

44. **Sunglasses & sunblock** – The sun continues to do more damage every year as our planet's protective atmosphere deteriorates. I notice quicker sunburns now than even when I first started hunting a little over a decade ago, so sunglasses and sunblock are usually in order. HINT: Though polarized sunglasses are helpful in screening out harmful rays for your eyes, they're not so great to use with some detectors. A few models have digital screen lenses that react strangely with polarized sunglasses, appearing wavy or with a rainbow pattern, making the display difficult to read. Try yours before wearing them on a hunt to make sure you won't have to deal with this annoyance.

45. **Spare socks** – If your feet sweat in warm weather, get cold in freezing weather, or wet at any time, a spare pair of dry socks can save the rest of your hunt. I recommend a breathable blend of cotton and synthetics.

46. **Bug spray and lip balm** – If your area is swampy, near any pools of standing water, or in the northern regions where "black fly season" is a thing, you know the value of bug spray. While many people swear by the DEET-saturated chemical formulas, I don't like putting that stuff on my skin.

   I've had fantastic luck using Avon's *Skin So Soft* pump spray. It's effective and comes in lightweight, thin and easy-to-pack plastic bottles. These are non-aerosol, so they're enviro-friendly and you don't have to worry about them exploding in an over-hot vehicle. *Off!* brand offers a formula that uses a mixture very much like *Skin So Soft*, but it doesn't smell as nice—something guys probably won't care about, but gals will likely appreciate, as I do.

A good quality lip balm can really provide comfort from dry, cracked lips if you're outside a while, especially in windy conditions. This may sound like a small thing, but having any part of your body in pain can really ruin what might otherwise be a fun outing. Be willing to spring for the good stuff, because while cheaper products may be good for immediate relief, they don't last long before you need to re-apply, which is a pain—especially with gloves on.

47. **Snake guards** – If you hunt regions where poisonous snakes are common, you definitely want to invest in some of these to protect your lower legs from snake strikes. Not only could a bite end your hunt in a very painful way; if it happens far enough out in the field where you can't reach medical help quickly, it could make you very sick and conceivably end your life.

48. **Snacks** – If you get hungry in the field, it's nice to have a few portable snacks to quickly quell the growl in your belly. Power bars, granola bars, nuts, anything with peanut butter and fruit are all good choices, not just for their almost instant energy boost, but also because they travel easy and keep well in a pouch or fanny pack. Again, it may seem like no big deal, but it's really annoying to be on a hot streak and suddenly be unable to focus because you're really hungry. It's distracting and keeps you from really enjoying yourself, so keep some non-perishable snacks in your vehicle's glove compartment and if you don't eat them right away, replace them occasionally.

Finding Hunting Spots

Finding places to hunt is probably the most challenging aspect of this hobby, and with more people getting into detecting every year, it's only going to get more difficult. Be that as it may, if you want to hunt anywhere other than your own yard, you need to learn how to identify, find and get permission to hunt other places.

49. **Start simple.** When you're just starting, the obvious choice is to start in your own yard. Regardless whether you live in a historic area or not, you want to start where you can mess up your holes before you get the hang of doing it right. Your yard also has the advantage of being convenient at any time, and you don't have to ask permission (unless you live in an apartment building and need to ask your landlord). If that's the case, and the landlord won't allow it, the next best place is a local park or playground. Municipal parks, playgrounds and school yards are paid for with tax dollars, so by being a taxpayer, you have a right to hunt those areas unless posted otherwise or covered by ordinances specifically prohibiting metal detecting.

50. **Do your homework.** Once you've got the hang of digging your holes as small as possible, the next thing you want to do to locate potential hunting spots is research. The more and better your research, the more and better spots you'll find. Good places to do your research include your local historical society and library. A good starting point would be microfilm/microfiche of old newspapers, and sometimes

there will be bound books of old historical lectures and presentation transcripts. In these, you can learn about what kinds of things happened in your area, and where they took place. Remember: In order to find things underground, they had to go into the ground to begin with. That means you want to find places where people gathered. The more physically active they were when there, the better chance they dropped something.

51. **Advanced Research** – You should also consult old maps of your area (the older, the better), also available at the historical society archives and local library. Don't overlook specialized libraries inside of museums, colleges and universities.

    Take advantage of the presence of any local historians, including the old guys that sit around in small cafés and general stores talking all day. Make friends, buy them a cuppa, and settle in to enjoy their stories. You can learn more from them than you might imagine, and they'll appreciate the chance to tell them to a fresh pair of ears.

    Your town's municipal office may have old tax maps from as far back as when your municipality was founded and/or incorporated. The specific department where they'll be archived varies from one place to another, but some of these include the Tax Assessor's Office, Register Of Deeds and Clerk of Courts.

52. **Online Research** – Another great source of maps and historic photos are websites, which will help you pinpoint the location of buildings, pools, etc.

    • The Library of Congress has some in their American Memories collection at LOC.gov.

- There are some great old topographic photos shot from airplanes starting in the 1930s at HistoricAerials.com and at VintageAerial.com.

- Old road and political maps, topographical maps and aerial photos are available at usgs.gov/pubprod/aerial.html

- Many municipalities, especially larger cities, have digitized their old tax maps and have made them available on their official websites, so just do a search to see if yours is online. These maps often show actual locations of dwellings, barns and outbuildings on residential properties; churches, schools and hospitals on institutional grounds; courthouses, jails, town halls and libraries on municipal tracts; and factories, stores and office buildings in commercial districts. Though these buildings may be long gone, whatever went into the ground when they were there is likely still waiting for you to find it.

Potential places to consider:

53. Residential, Agricultural & Commercial Properties

These are the easiest spots to find and get permission for. Look beyond what's there now, because buildings come and go and sometimes even get relocated. This is where your research will pay off, and old tax maps are your friends.

- **Clotheslines** – This is one of the best places to find old coins that fell out of pockets when shirts and pants were hung upside-down.

- **Fence posts & rails; field & property boundary walls** – People sat on, kneeled by, talked and jumped over and played on these walls and fences, and dropped things when they did.

- **Gardens & flower beds** – Kneeling to dig and weed caused dropped items.

- **Ghost towns** – If you can find one that hasn't been pounded to death, who knows what you might find?

- **Old barns and outbuildings** – These were often used for many purposes. Don't forget to check around foundations where jars of coins and other valuables may have been stashed because people didn't trust the banks.

- **Old homestead sites** – Watch for remaining chimneys, cellar holes & foundations

- **Taverns** – Drinking establishments and fights = lots of dropped articles, especially coins!

- **Vacant lots** – No telling what went on there.

- **Wells and outhouses** – Also used as trash receptacles, now prime treasure troves for the brave and patient with lots of energy and the tools to dig deep.

- **Yards and backyards** – Wherever people spent most of their time, that's where most things were dropped. You'll find the most old coins within 20-50 feet of a front porch or back door.

54. Institutional

- **Churches** – The older, the better. Look for ones whose grounds next to the building haven't been paved over.

- **College campuses** – Quads, greens and anywhere students lounged around or held recreational activities are prime hunting grounds.

- **Hospital grounds** – Generally, you can only hunt abandoned or former grounds, for safety and security reasons.

- **Schools** – Elementary, middle and high schools, and even one-room schoolhouses. Like churches, the older, the better; but even modern school grounds will contain some clad and other small treasures.

55. Public Activity Grounds & Recreational Areas

If places where people gather are ripe for hunting relics, coins and jewelry, then places where lots of people came together—especially when celebrating and having fun—can be considered prime treasure hunting spots.

- **Amusement parks** – Concession stands, coin toss booths, admission gates—anywhere people were pulling money from their pockets is where you'll find the greatest concentrations of old coins. Also around restrooms, game booths and rides like the Tilt-A-Whirl that whip around fast. Kids drop small prize items they won, all over the place.

- **Athletic fields** – Try to find out where old bleachers were located, since lots of things fell down between those seats; and don't forget the dugouts, ticket and concession stands.

- **Band shells** – When these were most popular, people sat on the ground on blankets to listen and dropped a lot of stuff getting up and down and playing with their kids. Still do.

- **Beaches** – This is a more specialized kind of metal detecting, with equipment, strategies and a lingo all its own. If you live near a beach, I strongly recommend getting one of the many books written specifically for beach hunters, and seek online info.

- **Campgrounds** – Lots of physical activity mixed with specialized gear and often an abundance of adult beverages = lots of potential dropped items.

- **Canal paths** – Before most of these became off-limits as part of national and state park systems, hundreds of thousands of people and animals trod the towpaths on either side, and the boats dropped things into the water. If you can gain legal access to either area, consider yourself very lucky and take advantage of it.

- **Circus/fair sites** – Lots of people, lots of animals, lots of activity; all fairly close together and not paying a lot of attention to their pockets.

- **City/town (municipal) parks** – Money falls out of pockets when kids play on the playground equipment. Sporting fields will also have pocket spills. I've found volleyball courts especially productive. County parks are the same, but more often have restrictions on metal detecting, so be sure you're allowed to hunt or you may get your equipment confiscated and never returned.

- **Drive-ins** – Especially in child play areas in front of or directly beneath the screen, and immediately around the concession stand and restrooms, you'll find the most items. Some old drive-ins also had coin-activated speakers, so the places where those speakers were mounted are hot spots for coins.

- **Fishing spots** – You'll find a lot of lead sinkers and fishing lures here, in addition to the usual coins, pocket knives and the occasional fishing pole.

- **Flea markets/swap meets** – Some of these areas are long-established, and these are endless sources of small dropped items and tons of coins. Also, due to the nature of what vendors sell there, you may find some more exotic objects.

- **Hiking trails** – Any time you mix strenuous physical activity and backpacks, you're going to find dropped articles.

- **Ice skating pond, creek & river banks** – If you've ever gotten onto or off of the ice in a place like this, you know why many things are dropped by ice skaters.

- **Picnic groves** – The older, the better. In the days before picnic tables, everyone spread a picnic blanket and ate on the ground. Getting up and down from that activity, as well as napping and playing games, provided many opportunities to drop things.

- **Playgrounds** – The ones covered with sand or wood chips are easy to dig and very often contain coins and small toys such as Matchbox-type cars.

- **Racetracks** – Horses. Excitement. Adult beverages. Need I say more? Hard to get permission, though.

- **Renaissance faires** – Aside from the many visitors—some of whom partake of too much grog or mead—there are lots of jugglers, jousters and other re-enactors who lose things all the time at these faires. There are also many vendor tents where coins and small pieces of jewelry fall to the ground.

- **Reunion areas** – Family reunions often happen in parks and community picnic grounds, but they can also happen in farmers' fields and other wide open spaces. It's helpful to read old newspapers' Society

Pages or Local News sections to find out where families held their celebrations. If you don't have ready access to your local historical society's archives, an annual subscription to Newspapers.com is affordable and convenient, allowing you to research old local papers any time. Just make sure this online service offers access to the papers you're interested in—they're adding new ones all the time as they get their collections scanned to digital.

- **Rodeo arenas** – Hunting under and around bleachers and fences where people gather to watch, as well as on the competition grounds themselves where riders—and the contents of their pockets—get bucked and thrown is usually quite productive.

- **Ski/tubing slopes** – Many things are dropped every year by people flying—and tumbling—downhill.

- **Swimming holes & swim spots along waterways** – Places where people strip off to swim and get re-dressed, or jump into the water with coins in their pockets and jewelry on their bodies, are primo hunting grounds. Look especially for areas with evidence of a rope swing: More acrobatic activity than normal means more items dropped from pockets.

- **Under seaside boardwalks** – Between the stuff (particularly coins) that falls through cracks in the boardwalk above and the stuff that falls out of the pockets of people engaged in activities below, these are fertile hunting grounds. This also makes them trashy, so using a small, "sniper" type coil can help you sniff out the good stuff in between the junk.

- **Walking/running trails** – These activities are synonymous with stuff falling out of pockets and day packs.

- **Winter sledding areas** – Sledding hills are noto-riously productive hunting grounds from all the stuff that gets catapulted out of pockets when sleds leave the ground over bumps and moguls, or overturn at the bottom of the hill.

56. Private Recreation Areas

You'll find similar items in these areas as you will at public recreation grounds, in addition to religious medals, fishing lures and sinkers, small hand tools, scouting accoutrements such as neckerchief slides and belt buckles, food preparation tools, and even a weapon or two.

- Church supper groves

- Fishing camps

- Hunting lodges and camps

- Scout camps

57. Travel Accommodations

Any place where people stopped in their travels is a place where they had to get in and out of vehicles, maybe had picnics, or waited to be picked up. All kinds of things have been inadver-tently dropped during these activities.

- **Areas adjacent to historical markers** – Popular stopping places for families with kids to take a break from the road and run around getting their ya-yas out...and dropping things.

- **Bridges and fords** – Especially in areas where there were ferry services or fords over waterways, many items were dropped from horses, or fell out of upset saddle bags, or bounced from vehi-cles over bridge rails and into the water, where they've been laying for decades or even centuries, just waiting for you to find them.

- **Lookout/scenic overlook sites** – People are often preoccupied with the view and trip over curbs or miss their pockets when putting things away. Check especially around coin-operated viewscopes.

- **Motels** – High-end hotels won't allow it, but more pedestrian motels often will. Still, try to be low-key about it and don't get in anyone's way or give them a reason to chase you off.

- **Old gas stations and general stores** – These have both been historically very popular gathering places for locals, and lots of time was spent hanging around porches and doorways.

- **Resorts** – Toys, jewelry, watches, pocket knives, sourvenirs, horseshoes (the game kind)

- **Roadside rest stops** – These can be very productive sites, especially near vending machines and in pet walking areas, but make sure there are no state laws against detecting there; laws vary from state to state.

58. Municipal Areas

NOTE: Theoretically, as a taxpayer, you should have the right to hunt municipal areas. However, with today's hyper-vigilant stance on security, you definitely need to ask permission, and it's a good idea to get it in writing in case you're approached about it. Especially good hunting when they're tearing up lots, streets and sidewalks for repair or replacement, but you have to be quick to get in there before they start building or paving.

- **Municipal Building Lots** – Town halls, police, library, etc. Be careful for lots of glass and can slaw.

- **Sidewalk Grassy Strips** – Between modern drops and whatever's in there from history, you'd be surprised what you can find, especially near parking meters and areas where plows deposit snow.

- **Town Squares, Greens & Commons** – Because these have generally been in use longer than other public areas, you have better chances of finding the good older stuff.

59. Rural Spots

Be aware that some of these are located on private property, so permission will need to be sought accordingly.

- **Churchyards & cemeteries** – Coins, jewelry, watches, religious medals

- **Farmers markets** – Coins, animal tack, farm tools

- **Lover's lanes** – Yeah, stuff gets dropped.

- **Roadside fruit and vegetable stands** – People drop coins all the time at these popular concessions, but you'll need the property owners' permission.

- **Roadside mailboxes** – The mail delivery person may drop coins, lighters or other objects here, as might the people picking up their mail.

- **Rural dance, religious baptism & revival sites** – Lots of physical activity takes place at these places, so chances of finding dropped items is high.

- **Waterfalls** – People have always stopped to view these natural wonders and even to drink from their waters, and usually had to climb or hike to do so. Things got dropped.

60. Historic & Military Sites

Generally, you'll only be able to hunt old abandoned or decommissioned military installations, and you must still get permission. All national and most state historic military and battle sites are off-limits to amateur detecting. The only way you might ever get to hunt these are under the guidance of official historic organizations, and then you'll have to turn over all your finds (but they're still fun to dig!). However, if you're a go-getter, you may be able to knock on a few surrounding residential doors to get some permissions on those properties.

- **Citizen militia drilling fields** – Most of the historic ones are located in the eastern quarter of our country, since that's what was settled the earliest, but there are still some militia drilling grounds outside that area. You can find everything from buckles and horse tack to coins, bullets and weapon parts. I've even found eating utensils and you may find military decorations (medals).

- **Battle sites** – A few of these from Revolutionary and Civil War battles remain outside national park jurisdiction. You'll need to do your research to find out where they are.

- **Military encampment sites** – Many of these from as early as the fur trade era are located away from protected historic sites. You will still have to get permission from landowners, but it's a lot easier than trying to get permission from the government.

- **Modern military installations** – Chances are, you'll only get to hunt one of these if you're stationed on it or know someone who is. If you do get permission, strictly obey all instructions and avoid restricted areas. They don't fool around in these days of high security risks.

- **Old forts** – Most are off-limits as historic sites, but there may still be some little-known local ones.

61. Disaster Sites

CAUTION: It's important to remember that many of these sites are places where people may have died, and often violently. Be sensitive when seeking permission in these areas, because those you're asking for permission may have lost someone they loved or significant property, such as their homes.

For this reason, I do NOT recommend trying to hunt a disaster site that's less than five years old (unless requested to by those who lost something), because anything else just too soon for people who have suffered such great losses. And let's face it: Unless you're there to help, showing up too soon after a disaster is tremendously insensitive and just kind of ghoulish. Karma counts: Don't be icky.

- **Beaches adjacent to shipwrecks** – Ancient coins, relics and even parts of old vessels still wash up on beaches, particularly following violent storms.

- **Plane crash areas** – Recovery crews always miss some items.

- **Roadsides where vehicles have wrecked** – Again, cleanup crews are in a hurry and often miss items. Be very, very careful not to place yourself in any danger of causing or becoming a victim of a new crash while hunting.

- **Tornado & hurricane damage paths** – No one will ever find everything flung about by these incredible storms. One account tells how the nephew of an Alabama tornado victim used his detector to find every heirloom ring mentioned in the victim's will so they could be distributed among her heirs as she wished. This is one time we, as detectorists, can go in soon after the event and offer a little bit of comfort to those who may have lost everything else they own. Please be good ambassadors by helping eagerly, with kindness and generosity.

62. Abandoned Sites

Any place where people once lived, worked or played but no longer do: These are great places to hunt, because what you find is likely to be old and/or historical, therefore more valuable. There will usually be few or no other people there to get in your way. If you find an abandoned site through research, chances are not many other people – if any – have hunted it before. CAUTION: On any industrial site, there is the possibility of encountering hazardous materials and situations, so make sure you get permission, ask what you might find there in terms of safety issues, and use great caution when you're onsite. This goes double for places containing scraped soil, which may or may not have been tested for toxic content. Regardless, always wear gloves and any other safety gear that might be appropriate for whatever you might expect to encounter.

- **Boundary lines** – where old walking, hiking or riding trails cross county or state boundaries – This is where maintenance workers would have ended their duties for the day or stopped to have lunch and maybe a nap or a quick game of catch. Things were dropped during these activities.

- **Junctions of old roads** no longer used. Crossroads have always been places where people got in and out of vehicles, stopped to rest or chat or turned and had thing shift and fall off their vehicles.

- **Mining camps** – Many metal objects are still being recovered from old mining camps to this day.

- **Old cemeteries in the woods** – These might be old churchyards, small public cemeteries or private graveyards originally located in fields or yards allowed to go wild, where forests have grown up around them. Always ask permission and NEVER dig directly around or over the graves, only on the borders (I try to stay at least five feet away from actual graves). Not only is digging on top of graves themselves illegal, it's deeply disrespectful and just bad Karma.

- **Old garbage dumps** – These can be full of surprising treasures as well as hazards. It's best to dig these with company, since you never know if you may fall into an unexpected void and need help back out, or experience an injury from sharp items. Always stay current on your tetanus shots.

- **Old stone quarries** – another place it's a good idea to hunt with a buddy, since most quarries were abandoned when the digging machines hit a natural spring and the giant hole filled up. There are lots of hidden dangers here.

- **Piles of scraped construction site soil** – Many people think scraping has removed all the "good stuff," but depending how far down they scraped, construction workers may have just moved it all into a convenient pile for you to explore!

- **Railroad grades, stations and junctions** – Lots of human activity took place along the tracks, and there was a lot of throwing of items to and from the trains.

Staying Legal

63. Every location has its own local ordinances, but usually state and federal laws will override local ordinances on nationally designated areas such as parks and recreation areas. If you don't know if hunting is allowed and don't know where to find out, consider them off-limits; better safe than sorry.

64. Theoretically, unless it's posted otherwise, you can hunt on public property. That said, you want to be very careful, because hunting on certain property can get you a fine and immediate, permanent confiscation of your equipment with no compensation to you. It's really best to find out who owns the property and take the time to ask permission.

65. Where you park your vehicle when hunting can have as much legal ramification as where you hunt. Make sure you're allowed to park where you want to, or you may return to a towed vehicle that's nowhere to be seen. NOT a fun way to end your hunt.

Getting permission

66. **Just do it.** As a rule, you cannot hunt private property unless given express permission by the landowner. Yes, there are people who do so, but they are no friend to you or to me, nor to the hobby. They are breaking the law and the Digger's Code of Ethics, and they are contributing to the increasing public perception that treasure hunters are just a bunch of disrespectful pirates out to rape the land and steal from people.

67. **Calling cards.** Carrying a calling card with my name, phone number and a list of things I find was a game-changer for me in the permission-getting game. It just seems to impart another level of professionalism, credibility and that results in more trust. I know for a fact that giving out my card has turned several conversations that were headed in the "no" direction into "yeses." My card also says "Call me if you lose something in your yard." It has a cartoonish, humorous drawing of me on it and it's in bright, friendly colors. I always have some in my car and even if

someone tells me no when I ask permission, I leave one with them. I say, "I understand, thanks anyway. But hang onto this. If you ever lose something, give me a call. I'll come help you find it." I don't charge people for this service, but I do ask permission to hunt the rest of their property, and I've never had someone turn me down in that situation. After all, I've helped them find something of value to them, and didn't ask for any payment in return. One favor deserves another, right? You can buy high quality, full-color calling cards affordably at Vistaprint.com.

68. **Timing is everything.** It's easier by far to ask for permission from someone you're already talking to about something else, especially something you have in common. For this reason, it's best when "cold calling" to wait until you see someone outside in their yard. This way, you know you're not interrupting them in the middle of doing something important, because you can see what they're doing, and you don't have to knock on a door.

If they live in an old house, it's a safe bet they're people who love history, because otherwise an old house is just an expensive place to live that requires a lot of care. That being the case, pull up and say hi, be friendly, and tell them you admire their home and property, that you're a history buff, and ask how old the place is, how long it's been in the family, etc.

Soon you'll be having a genuinely enjoyable conversation, and it will likely lead to a natural opportunity to tell the person you're a metal detectorist and ask for permission. Once they know you love and respect history as they do, they're far more likely to give you permission.

69. **Establish trust.** I also make sure to tell them clearly, "I fill all my holes and don't leave your yard a mess," very directly, because that is what they're most worried about. Let them know you'll respect any boundaries they set for off-limits areas, and offer to show them whatever you find. If you think there's any chance you might be challenged by neighbors or someone else, ask if you could get permission in writing. Be careful though, because you don't want to trigger a "no" by making them think too much about it.

70. **Details matter.** Ask if there are any areas of their property they'd rather you didn't go. Ask if there are any buried electrical lines, invisible dog fences or other hazards, and stay away from those. (The invisible fence will cause such interference, you probably won't be able to hunt anyway unless your sensitivity is turned almost all the way down.) Ask where their septic tank is buried, if they have one, and stay away from that, too. Also, make sure you're aware of any pets that you may encounter. If they have a dog running loose, ask them to introduce you to it and make friends before trying to hunt. Otherwise, the dog will just be doing its job if it senses you're an invader and it tries to run you off.

Hunting

There are many, many things to know about the hunting itself, to the point that I'm still learning after a dozen years in the hobby. I don't think I'll ever learn it all, but I keep my eyes and ears open and notice things as much as possible, and urge you to do the same. I'm just going to mention a few things that I think are really important when you're just starting out, because you don't know what you don't know, and sometimes what you don't know really can hurt you.

71. **It pays to dig all targets** until you learn your machine's individual signal tones. There's just no better way to do it.

72. **Grid off large parcels** into smaller, more manageable sections, then search them methodically, to cover all ground. You can mark off areas with branches and other stuff you find around the area.

73. **Overlap the ends of your sweeps** to make sure you don't miss anything. It only takes a fraction of an inch to miss an incredible find.

74. **With search coils, size matters:** the larger they are, the deeper they read. But you may need a smaller one to get in between the junk in trashy areas with lots of iron and foil.

75. **Don't jam your digger into the ground right above your target.** Move your digger several inches away from where the target is and start digging around it. This is how you make a plug. Dig almost all the way around it, leaving just a small flap of turf holding

onto the plug, which will act like a hinge to hold it in place when you flip it out of the hole. This way, it'll be easy to replace, and you won't accidentally hit your target and damage it.

76. **If the ground's dry and hard, it's not a good idea to dig.** First of all, there's not enough moisture to hold a plug together well so you can make a clean recovery and replacement. Most importantly, if the soil's that dry, you'll likely kill any grass above your hole, so unless you're out in a field, just wait for some rain.

77. **Lazy digging can be good.** For instance, when digging a plug on a hill, cut it so gravity does most of the work keeping the plug out of your way as you dig. Similarly, when digging a plug, it's helpful to angle the cut to allow the most light to enter the hole. This is most true when the sun is lower toward the horizon, so you can see what you're digging better. And when your knees and legs are tired, it's easier to get up from a squat if you face uphill.

Note the pyramid or squat cone shape of the plug. It has been dug at an angle toward the target, but careful to avoid hitting it. It's been flipped on a turf "hinge" right next to the hole, so it can be easily flopped back into place and tamped down neatly with a foot.

– Photo by author

Above: Especially when the sun is at a low angle in the sky, it's helpful to be able to see farther into the hole if you dig your plug so the turf hinge flips away from the sun. This will keep your plug from blocking its rays, so as much light as possible enters the hole.

Below: When digging on a hill, try to remember to position the turf hinge on the downside of the hole. This way, gravity will work with you in flipping the plug away from the hole, instead of wanting to flip it back into it while you're digging, which can be very annoying.

– Illustrations by the author

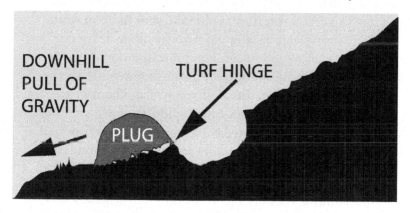

DOWNHILL
PULL OF
GRAVITY

TURF HINGE

PLUG

78. **Always re-check your holes** before you fill them in. There may be more than one target in there!

Safety

79. **Dummy Digging** – If you're on a developed property that contains buildings, you're on property that likely contains buried electrical, water and maybe septic lines. Your detector will pick these up, along with metal well cover plates and other similar items. If you're getting a strong signal, and it looks like it could be in a place where an electrical line might be, run your detector around it in all directions. If you pick up a continuous signal in any direction, it's a line of some sort. Don't be a digging dummy: Unless you want to call the local digging hotline, just move on to the next signal. Not worth the hassle and danger.

80. **Headphones** – If you hunt by yourself away from other people, it's best not to wear your headphones over both ears. Unfortunately, some people will see you alone and take advantage of the fact that you're concentrating on the ground and not your environment, and sneak up behind you. At best, they may knock you out, take your wallet, keys and equipment and leave you to wake up to a sad and scary situation. At worst, they could take your life. Not worth hearing a faint signal, so if you're alone, leave one earmuff off so you can maintain situational awareness. You also want to be aware of any wild animals that may pose a threat. If you live and hunt in an area where you know bears, wildcats, wolves or other large carnivores have been seen, look up and around you every once in a while and again, leave one ear free to hear them.

81. **Hunting Alone** – The truth is that in general, if you metal detect alone, you are vulnerable, careful though you may be. Especially when you're far out in the back country, it's always best to hunt with a friend if

at all possible. Some diggers like to bring their dogs along. It's a great idea, as they're usually hyper-vigilant and can alert you to approaching danger long before you'd know it's near. Just be sure to bring along enough water to keep your pup hydrated and some food if you're going to be out past mealtime. And some diggers do carry firearms to protect themselves from wild animals and wild people.

82. **Hydrate and Communicate** – I know I mentioned these both before, but they're worth repeating: Drink enough water and keep a charged cell phone with you. Keep several jugs or bottles of water with you, not just soda or beer or caffeinated drinks. Sugar, alcohol and caffeine are all natural dehydrators. Water is what you need to stay hydrated, and that phone could be your best friend if you encounter a flat tire, dead battery or worse. No hunt is worth risking your life, so play safe. If you must hunt alone, tell someone where you're going and when you expect to return.

83. **Severe Weather** – I'm constantly amazed at how many detectorists go hunting without checking the forecast. I'm not saying don't hunt if there's a chance for rain, but if there's any possibility you could encounter thunderstorms and lightning (remember, you're out in the middle of a field waving a metal stick around!), flooding rains, tornadoes, or sudden-onset winter storms, make sure you're prepared. Load a good weather app with decent radar and a lightning indicator on your smartphone, and check it before you go afield. WeatherBug is the best overall free app, and keeps getting better, I think. And just look up from the ground to check the sky every so often. Seriously, there's no excuse to be surprised by bad weather these days.

Courtesy & Etiquette

84. **There is actually an accepted code of ethics** among most metal detectorists. Not all diggers follow it, but the ones who don't are the ones who make it difficult for the rest of us to find people willing to let us hunt their properties. Don't be one of these jerks, who ruin the hobby for everyone.

~ Metal Detectorist's Code of Ethics ~

This is one version of the code, but they're all pretty much the same. PLEASE be a good ambassador for our hobby and make it easier for yourself and other detectorists to get new permissions, by following this code of ethics for respecting nature, history and property owners.

- I will respect private property and will not metal detect without the property owner's permission.

- I will not destroy property, buildings, or what is left of ghost towns and deserted structures.

- I will never litter, always pack out what I take in, and remove all trash found.

- I will leave all gates and other accesses to land as found.

- I will not damage natural resources, wildlife habitats, or any private property.

- I will use thoughtfulness, consideration, and courtesy at all times.

- I will abide by all laws, ordinances, or regulations that may govern my search or the area I will be in.

- I will fill all plugs, regardless of how remote the location, and never dig in a way that will damage, be damaging to, or kill any vegetation.

- I will report the discovery of items of significant historical value to a local historian or museum in accordance with the latest legislation.

- I will be a positive ambassador for the metal detecting hobby.

When in public, be polite and informative to those who inquire about your hobby. Remember—you are an ambassador of a pastime we all want to preserve, and other detectorists will be judged by how you act and respond.

Other etiquette points:

85. **Don't ask, don't tell** – It's bad form to ask another digger where they hunt, beyond just general locations. No one wants to give up their spots, and it's rude to put them into the position of having to say so. And if someone invites you to hunt one of their spots, reciprocate, even if yours aren't as good. Similarly, just because you went to hunt one of their spots with someone as their guest doesn't mean you should go there without them. You shouldn't.

86. **Whoever digs it, keeps it.** So if someone locates a target with their detector but someone else digs it, it belongs to the digger, not the finder. But you should only ever dig someone else's location if they tell you it's okay, if you asked them to help you find something, or if you're tag-teaming the hunt.

87. **It's not a competition** unless you want it to be. It's about finding history and learning more about the past, and spending time with people who enjoy the

same hobby. If you're in it for money or glory, you're going to be sorely disappointed.

88. **There's no whining in treasure hunting.** Sometimes the day is beautiful and fun and you find lots of great stuff. Sometimes it's rainy and cold and you only find rusty nails and pulltabs. That's part of the deal, so don't make it worse for yourself and anyone you may be hunting with by getting whiny or grumpy about it.

89. **There is no "best detector of all."** Each does things a little differently according to what specialty it's built for. It's okay to be proud of your own detector, but running down someone else's machine makes you a jerk.

90. **You don't want to hunt too close to someone else,** because when two detectors get close together, they tend to make each other act wonky. As a general rule, stay at least ten feet away from anyone else with a live machine.

Fun - Buddies, Clubs and Organized Hunts

91. **Some folks like to hunt alone,** others prefer the social aspect of hunting in a group. I enjoy both. When I first started hunting, you had to know where to look to find others to hunt with. Now, it's fairly easy: There are tons of detecting pages and groups on Facebook, and there are still several full websites dedicated to detecting and other forms of treasure hunting. A simple Web search will find more than you can probably count.

92. **There are many clubs** of people who get together often to hunt, and many of these have dedicated websites and/or Facebook pages. Most of them welcome new members, and some of them host group hunts once or twice a year. Again, most of them can be found

through a Web search. Not surprisingly, these tend to be geographically based. I encourage you to join one of these clubs if you're lucky enough to have one in your area. Not only will you learn a lot about metal detecting a lot faster than you would otherwise, you'll learn a lot more about your community, its people and its history. What's not to like?

93. **Group hunts:** I'm not going to go deeply into this subject because it could probably warrant a small book of its own, but you should know there are two major kinds of group hunts: organic and seeded.

    Organic hunts are the kind where the host finds a property to hunt, then people pay money to compensate the land owner and to cover expenses such as lunch, a porta-potty onsite and maybe some prizes for various things such as oldest item, most valuable coin, deepest recovery, etc. There are no guarantees you'll find anything, but there's generally a guarantee that the property hasn't been hunted before and there's a good likelihood there are some old things in the ground.

    Seeded hunts are those where there's a guarantee something good is in the ground, because the hunt producers planted or "seeded" items on the property. There are many ways this can happen, but generally a lot of people find good stuff because it was put there for that purpose. There are often multiple different hunt sessions for specific items, such as relics or silver coins or big coppers, during a single event.

Weird Stuff

Depending on where you live and hunt, sooner or later you're going to encounter something funky that doesn't seem to make any sense with your detector. This doesn't mean there's anything wrong with your machine, it may just be some rather common natural phenomena that affects electrical or magnetic fields, which is what your machine actually detects: a disruption in electrical auras, not actually the item itself. Some of the more common weird things you'll eventually run into include (but are not limited to):

94. **Falsing** – This is the term given to the tendency of any metal detecting machine to produce signal tones where there aren't really any targets beneath your coil. There are many causes for falsing:

    • Stray electrical charges from overhead wires, high tension lines or underground electrical lines

    • Highly mineralized soil

    • Actual "misfiring" of your machine or pinpointer due to something broken or shorting out. If you consistently encounter falsing and there don't seem to be any environmental causes, you may want to have the manufacturer check it out for operational problems.

95. **Mineralization** – This happens in soil that is high in certain naturally occurring substances such as iron. The dirt itself may be so highly charged that it emits its own low-key magnetic signal that can cause your machine to "chatter" or emit a constant stream of annoying sounds that don't indicate real targets but can indeed obscure deep or weak signals. It can get downright maddening, and the only thing you can do is try to ground balance for the soil, and/or turn down the sensitivity on your machine. This effect will be worse in damp or moist soil, such as just after a rainfall.

96. **Hot Rocks** – These are what otherwise look like normal rocks, but which will repeatedly create a signal tone just as if they were legitimate targets.

They tend to occur in highly mineralized ground, and they can take various forms. Where I live along the East Coast, the soil has ultra high iron content, and this seems to turn ordinary rocks into "hot rocks."

More often than not, the rocks here in Eastern Pennsylvania appear to be some form of coal: shiny gray-black with the look almost of squared-off crystal edges, and quite a bit lighter in weight than other rocks their size. I guarantee the first time you find one, it will make you feel foolish, but it's not just you—we all get fooled by these little imposters.

They are worthless and not to be confused with meteorites, which are genuinely "hot" because they have some metal content from outer space; they also have considerable monetary value if you can prove they're really meteorites.

97. **Halo Effect** – This is the tendency of an object that's been in the ground a long time to develop an electrical "aura" around it that's either much larger than the object itself, or that indicates it's made of a different kind of metal than it actually is. It happens through a combination of exposure to the elements in the soil that may eventually change the chemical composition of the original metal, or simply a heavy deposit of oxidation.

This phenomenon occurs a lot with old iron, but it's most prominent with old aluminum cans. These generate such a huge halo effect that if they're within 6-8 inches of the surface, they can throw off a signal so huge and loud that if you're wearing headphones, it may feel like your eardrums are exploding.

Finds

98. **Cleaning** – This is another subject that can (and probably should and maybe does) have its own book, but there are a few very important basics you should know in the beginning.

- First, don't be tempted to rub the dirt off of your finds in the field, because if you have a valuable coin, that's the fastest way to ruin it. Just a few little surface scratches can rapidly devalue an old coin.

- Second, when you get them home, clean them only with water and mild dish soap, and maybe a soft toothbrush.

- Third, if the dirt is stubborn, soak the item in olive oil and check on it in a week or so. There are other tricks, especially to clean coins, but that's for a more advanced book.

The most important thing to know is that too much cleaning of an old coin can and will serious lessen its value, so make sure what you're doing before you do it. The best approach is to do just the minimum necessary to identify the coin until you know exactly what you're doing. You can always do more, but once you've ruined its value, there's no going back. Err on the side of caution. There are plenty of places online to learn how to properly clean a coin. I recommend starting on YouTube.

99. **Photographing** – Some folks like to record of their whole field experience, so they make videos of the

hunt, the digging and the recovery, then show the cleaned item with some identifying information. Others just enjoy taking still photos of the target once it's recovered.

Either way, you'll want to either use the camera in your smartphone, a handheld digital camera, or a fancy hat-mounted one such as a GoPro. If you're an underwater hunter, you'll need a water-proof housing for whatever you're using to record your hunt and/or finds. Most diggers get a bracket to mount it on the bill of their cap, to keep their hands free, because you've already got a detector in one hand and a digger or pinpointer in the other.

Most digital cameras give you the helpful option to tag your files with a date and location, which you can set up in its options menu. If you post photos of your finds online, try to make them either very close up, or shoot from an angle that will keep identifying details out of the shot, if you want to keep your best spots to yourself.

100. **Preserving** – This is another topic that deserves plenty more space, so I'll again just mention the most important stuff for beginners: Once you dig something out of the ground, especially if it's a century or more old, it will begin oxidizing the moment it hits the air. The soil has done a certain amount of preservation until then. So once you get the item cleaned and dried, there are a few options you must exercise. For coins, at the very least put them in cardboard mounts with the protective plastic windows. I like these because the mounts have plenty of room to record find date, location and anything else you want to remember about it. Some folks like to lightly oil them first.

For smaller relics that you've been able to clean down to the bare metal, it's helpful to give them a coat of microcrystalline Renaissance Wax, applied with a soft cotton cloth. Museums use this to preserve items in their collections. It's not cheap, but you can easily get it online through Amazon.com or eBay.

For small to medium-sized relics thickly encrusted with oxidation, you'll need to set up an electrolysis operation. This entails use of a battery or battery charger, alligator clips, plastic tubs full of a mixed solution, and a grounding item. Simply do a Web search to find excellent instructions, or YouTube for video tutorials. There are many out there. Larger encrusted items will either have to be sand-blasted (if they're not valuable) or dunked in larger electrolysis setups such as those found in museums or the locations of professional treasure hunters.

101. **Displaying** – There are many ways to display your finds, and the best way to get ideas is simply to visit other treasure hunters or their websites. But for the average beginner, the two best ways are to use a curio cabinet of some sort with lots of shelves and plenty of glass to see through, or to buy flat Riker Boxes or cases and arrange your finds between their soft, white stuffing layer and their glass lids. You've seen these boxes if you've ever gone to a swap meet or coin show. You can find them for purchase in many places online, including eBay, Amazon, and at hobby retailers. I get mine from RikerMounts. net because of their reasonable prices, excellent selection and related accessories all in one place, and friendly customer service.

BONUS SECTION – Resources

Unlike when I started detecting, there are way too many resources out there now to list here. Most are right at your fingertips or the click of a mouse on the Internet, and I encourage you to do some searching (especially for equipment dealers and manufacturers, who do a very good job promoting themselves). The resources I list here are a selection of those I've used myself and can recommend with some authority.

Again, this is not meant as a comprehensive list by any means, and omission of any you may know about is not intended to slight anyone. I'm just sharing what I have personally learned and used and can vouch for. But don't limit yourself: definitely spend some time online and amaze yourself with all the information that's out there for you.

One evolution of detecting I can report on—because I have been part of it and witnessed it myself—is the move from almost no available information to more than you might imagine. In a very short time, what you could find went from manufacturers' books and a few on narrow niches within the hobby—which you could really only find at metal detector retailers—to forum-based detecting communities to concentrations of social media pages and a plethora of blogs and niched websites.

This explosion has really all occurred over the past decade. Many of the detecting websites I frequented when the Internet was first maturing are now gone, with most of their members having migrated to the far more flexible and user-friendly, massive social interface created by Mark Zuckerberg.

I am beginning to see a move in the opposite direction, with some of the more popular Facebook personalities creating their own full websites and blogs. Some have also created YouTube video channels that have become wildly popular.

I use them all to one extent or another, along with the two more traditional media, books and magazines. Though I do often read nonfiction how-to titles in eBook format, I still prefer my magazines in print, not least because I enjoy sharing them with my digger pals who may subscribe to different titles. We then swap so we can all read everything, and that's still hard to do with digital editions. Not everyone owns a tablet…at least not yet. I'm sure that will change, too. Meanwhile, I'm publishing this book in print and digital, so everyone can consume its content according to their preference.

Meanwhile, as promised, here are my recommendations for other great sources of credible information for the detecting newbie:

How-To Information

Truly, you can't start in a better place than in the user manual that came with your detector. That's the exact information you need about

- how to operate it

- what its features are

- what they do and how they do it

- and the kind of performance you can expect.

Some models now also come with a DVD or a link in the manual to more information online at the manufacturer's website. I cannot recommend strongly enough that you read through your entire user manual at least once, and watch any video instructions at least twice or three times before ever taking your machine for its first spin.

But I've been at this a while, and I know most of you won't even do this once. So let me just remind you that when you get frustrated and feel like throwing your detector in the trash or worse, your manual and user DVD will always be there, waiting for you to do what you should have done in the first place.

Just sayin'.

Treasure Hunting Websites

There are new websites popping up every month, it seems, about every aspect of metal detecting and other forms of treasure hunting. Many catch on and become very popular, while other disappear just as quickly. It would be silly to try to keep up with them all in any print book, so just use "metal detecting" or "treasure hunting" as search terms when looking for them online.

Social Media Sites

There are several social media channels used by detectorists to find each other, network and socialize. Facebook is by far the most popular and ever-growing, because it's so easy to create a page, group or community and instantly start sharing. You can find one for just about every niche of treasure hunting imaginable. I've seen and used Pinterest pages about detecting, and as previously mentioned, YouTube is chock-full of great vids (and some other ...uh...interesting ones).

I've heard there's a growing presence for metal detecting on Instagram, but I'm not there...yet. And who knows what new social channels will pop up next?

Again, the following list is far from complete, but here are the pages and channels I can knowledgeably recommend, because I use and enjoy them myself.

CAUTION: Where there is any level of competition among people, you will find trolls (negative nasties whose sole enjoyment seems to come from spewing misery over any space where it seems people might be enjoying themselves). Facebook is no exception. In fact, it's probably one of the most prolific troll breeding grounds I know. But don't let that stop you: There are thousands of truly wonderful detectorists on Facebook; kind, generous with their knowledge, and there to support you when you're frustrated, confused or just don't know what to do as you start out in this hobby. Gravitate to them, follow their lead in behavior, and just ignore the ick. Trolls thrive on any kind of attention, and will eventually go away if we don't feed into that.

Facebook

Though there are many, many detecting-oriented FB pages, this is a list of only those pages and groups I have joined or follow. I have purposely not mentioned any secret groups—because if they wanted others to know about them, they wouldn't be secret—but I do belong to a few. I mention a few regional pages and groups here, and they exist for nearly every geographic region of the United States; find the ones near you and jump in!

Metal Detecting & Treasure Hunting – This is a very general Community page, owned by me. At the time of this writing, we have almost 2,400 followers who stop by to share their finds, post hunt videos, ask and answer questions, and enjoy the content I post related to treasure hunting around the world. It's an open forum with an international crowd, so just c'mon in and hang around a while. You're bound to learn a lot and meet some cool diggers who may turn into friends.

Crazy About Coins – A fun and generous group of coin and history enthusiasts. If you need help with coin or token identification, there are people here who can help you determine the nature of your finds.

History Resurfaced/Show and Tell – This public group is a great place, especially if you hunt alone and don't know any veteran diggers. You can post photos of your finds from current hunts, as long as it's artifact-related.

ID Me – A closed group but you can ask to join. I love this one, a very active group where people come to post photos of their finds and ask for help identifying what they've discovered. There are more than 4,000 members, which is very helpful because chances are that in a group of that size, someone has seen something like your item, if not the exact thing itself. Identifying finds is definitely a numbers game, with chances for success accurately naming your item higher with each person participating.

Women Diggers – This is my absolute favorite Facebook group, helmed by the enthusiastic and gracious Carla Autin. Yes, it's only open to women, because this hobby is still about 95% men and things can get very competitive and sometimes downright nasty on open, mixed pages. In Women Diggers land, we have rules of welcoming behavior, kindness and genuine support for other members, or you get the boot and will not be allowed back in. I've learned a lot here, and truly enjoy the company of my Dig Sisters. You must be invited by an existing member to join this group. Carla also blogs at "Flea's Diggin' Scoop" on her companion website, WomenDiggers.com.

Dirt Digging PA – Just what it sounds like, this is a closed group of nearly 1,300 members at the time of this writing. It's a general interest group for Pennsylvania-based diggers. As you might guess, a good bit of the discussion there is about good places to hunt in the Keystone State. It has a list of people who've made their locations known in case anyone nearby is looking for a hunt buddy. Friendly bunch!

Tri-State Hunters Inc. Metal Detecting – This is a group for those in the Pennsylvania, New Jersey, and Delaware/Maryland areas, but people from outside this region are free to join. Whether you're a coinshooter and dirt digger, a beach hunter or maybe into finding relics, everyone is welcome. They like it if you post your finds after a hunt. You can also find this group on MetalDetectingForum.com.

American History Metal Detecting – A companion page to the AmericanHistoryMetalDetecting.com website, this is an open, free-to-join group, meaning any member can add others. Don Westbrook founded this group to help others with their metal detecting endeavors. If you have any questions about anything metal detecting-related, feel free to ask…someone here will be able to help you. There are sometimes giveaways of related items in this group, and if you post finds and stories here to be discovered, you may find them posted on the American History Metal Detecting website!

Relic Recoverist Group – This closed group run by Jocelyn Elizabeth is dedicated to the distribution of knowledge, the sharing of experience, and the discovering of history. Members are encouraged to share their passion for the hobby and the treasures they may find along the way.

Detect America – This is a closed group, meaning you have to be added/invited by an existing member. Some of the most experienced and accomplished people in the hobby are members here, and you'll learn a lot, but I'd recommend starting with some of the open groups and pages first. Much of this discussion will be over your head and just frustrate you. You'll know when you're ready to move up to the big leagues.

Pinterest

Metal Detecting and Treasure Hunting! [pinterest.com/wildheart61/metal-detecting] – This is my Pinterest MD board. Not necessarily aimed at beginners (though there's a good bit of beginner-interest stuff there, along with some cool relic identification guides), just a collection of cool treasure hunting stuff. I try to focus on sharing cool new tips and tools, including research.

Sally May Kinsey's Treasure Stories [pinterest.com/SallyMayKinsey/treasure-stories] – Not specifically for the beginner, this board nevertheless has some truly cool and quirky stuff for anyone who enjoys treasure hunting.

Sophia Fuller's Metal Detecting Finds [pinterest.com/sophiatfuller/metal-detector-finds] – A diverse collection of pins about all aspects of metal detecting. Some really solid info on identifying, cleaning and preserving relics. The beginner will find a lot to follow down on this interesting board, for every type of hunter.

JP Fenwick's Metal Detecting [pinterest.com/jpfenwick/metal-detecting] – A wide variety of different treasure hunting pins from all over the Web. An emphasis on gold prospecting. Very informative.

Blogs

There are many, many of these, but I'm only going to list the ones I actually know, like and use. Most of them also maintain a presence on other prominent social media channels. You will notice that I include quite a few women-owned sites, because... well, I'm a woman, and it's kinda hard to find each other in this overwhelmingly male hobby. That makes it doubly hard for gals just getting started, so please indulge me. I also limited these to blogs that are regularly updated. Use these as a starting place only, and let their mentions and blogrolls help you find others that you'll use and enjoy. There are just a ton of them out there.

Detecting101.com – This is the companion site to this book, owned and maintained by me. I invite your questions and comments to keep it relevant to what you want and need to know about detecting information for the beginner.

DetectingDiva.com – I love this blog, and the whole site. I'll just let Allyson, a passionate digger, describe it herself: "Since I couldn't find a website which catered to, or even acknowledged, the female detectorist (aka detectorista), I decided to create one myself to share experiences, knowledge, finds and photos with other detectoristas. Of course men are welcome here, too—my machine discriminates, but I don't." Gotta love it!

Dirt Girl Unleashed [http://dirtgirlmetaldetecting.blogspot.com] – Whit Hill doesn't blog regularly, but when she does, it's worth reading. She lives and hunts around Nashville, Tennessee, in the heart of Civil War country, so her finds are never boring. Her blog offers a blogroll of some other sites you can explore. Whit has also released a music CD titled "I Dug It Up," featuring songs solely about metal detecting. You can listen to the songs on her video at https://www.youtube.com/watch?v=clvPAdohVVA, and you can buy the CD at http://www.cdbaby.com/cd/whithill3. I seriously love this CD and believe you will, too. I mean, who else is singing our songs?

DJDigs.net – An excellent and wide-ranging blog about every aspect of our hobby from D.J. Yost, an experienced and respected detecting veteran. He's also a dear friend, who happened to write the foreword for this guidebook.

Girls Rock Metal Detecting [http://girlsrockmetaldetecting.blog-spot.com] – Unabashed passion and pride among women metal detectorists from Siren Kimmie. This girl has a singularly enthusiastic personal style, and she can get out there and dig with the best of 'em.

MetalDetector.com [http://blog.metaldetector.com] – There is a LOT of great info here, and several other pages on the site, as well. Much of it is geared toward beginners, but there's enough here to move you along when you're ready, including a Community section, a Learn area with articles, reviews, manuals and videos, and a store where you can buy detectors and related gear.

RelicRecoverist.com – A wide-ranging and often humorous blog by Jocelyn Elizabeth, a young mom in central Pennsylvania who loves the picking life (finding and re-selling antiques and collectibles) and metal detecting. She shares her adventures alone and with her kids and other diggers, and her stories are never boring.

Stout Standards – [http://stoutstandards.wordpress.com] – This is really a full website that includes a blog, and a fantastic blogroll of other sites in which you may be interested. Dick Stout is one of the longtime champions of our hobby, and I strongly recommend you check out his books and all the great material on this site. It'll take you a long time to get through it; time well spent!

YouTube Channels

Again, there are many of these, but I've found a few that are either particularly interesting, informative, entertaining or all three. Here they are, and again, I encourage you to cruise around YouTube to find others you might like:

Aquachigger – Veteran detectorist Beau Ouimette takes us along on his adventures in the Southeastern US, metal detecting, treasure hunting, appreciating nature and critters. He's a very knowledgeable hunter and, as the name suggests, spends a lot of time in the water. It was after watching his vids that I decided to have a go at water detecting myself, and I'm still getting started with that. But I can't think of anyone else whose videos you can learn more from while truly enjoying the visuals and the voiceover. I also appreciate that Beau is critter-friendly and environmentally aware and concerned. I would seriously miss this channel if it were ever to go away.

NuggetNoggin – This was the first YouTube channel I ever subscribed to. Young Michael Bennett posts fantastic videos of his adventures afield with his detector (and sometimes detectorist friends). He often goes out in his southern location on foot, via ATV or in his kayak, and the results are always interesting, informative and enjoyable.

Relic News – News coverage by Laurie Gagne of amazing people and finds from metal detecting and treasure hunting. Some of the biggest names in the hobby are interviewed, sharing great stories and immense knowledge with all of us lucky enough to follow the channel.

The SilverSlingers – Dominique Ivy Da Silva and Mark Durant take us along on their frequent, energetic hunts through all the seasons of their New England region, from farm fields to cellar holes, residential yards to deep in the forest. They share some of the oldest and coolest finds you'll see on this continent!

Clubs

The only club I belonged to was short-lived, but there are several places where you can find hunt clubs in your area that you may wish to join. Here are a few of those dedicated to general metal detecting, but there are groups that specialize, such as gold prospecting, which I don't list here:

Federation of Metal Detector & Archaeological Clubs, Inc. – http://www.fmdac.org/clubs.html – Part of a whole site devoted to this non-profit group dedicated to legislative lobbying and education for the preservation, promotion, and protection for the hobby of recreational metal detecting and prospecting. Lists affiliated clubs.

MetalDetector.com – http://clubs.metaldetector.com/ – This useful site lets you find a club near you by state or GPS coordinates, then displays it on a Google map so you can get directions to meetings. Includes clubs for coin collectors and scuba divers.

Metal Detecting Clubs – http://www.metaldetectingclubs.org/ – Browse the list of clubs by state and see them indicated on a Google map. Includes tips for finding sites to hunt, and a thorough but not overwhelming Resources page. On there, you can find a Guide for Beginners, which lists a LOT of really helpful links for those just starting out.

Metal Detecting in the USA – http://www.metaldetectingintheusa.com/metal-detecting-clubs.html – Clubs listed by state, for the general metal detectorist, gold prospector and related interest groups. This is a full site with many other topics, including a Tips page and downloadable tip sheets.

Other Books

I have to admit to not having read all these books myself, but I feel it's my job in this quickstart guide to let you know of full-length books aimed at beginning detectorists. They're a lot more "meaty" than this guide, for after you've been out hunting a while and start to have some specific questions and need some in-depth answers. I can't vouch for quality, but here are the ones I've found that appear targeted to the beginner:

Metal Detecting:
A Beginner's Guide to Mastering the Greatest Hobby In the World
by Mark Smith
Published 2014 by CreateSpace
4.25 out of 5 stars
Seller's description: While this metal detecting book may be geared towards the novice treasure hunter, there are plenty of choice tips that even experienced treasure hunters can pick up. Mark Smith reveals some of his best guarded metal detecting secrets in this metal detecting guide that puts more treasure in your finds pouch. Fully illustrated diagrams and real life pictures describe in detail the easiest ways to not only locate treasure, but safely recover it as well.

Metal Detecting for Beginners and Beyond
by Tim Kerber
Published 2014 on Lulu Press, Inc.
3.6 out of 5 stars
Seller's description: This book will help quickly teach you how to not only start but excel at metal detecting. Tips, techniques and photos start with the basics (equipment choices if you don't have a machine yet) and quickly gets into specific tactics to maximize success regardless of what detector you are using. It has the "need to know" information to help you that would normally take you years to discover on your own. There is also a robust list of resources for your reference for more in-depth learning.

Metal Detecting for the Beginner
by Vince Migliore
Published 2009 by CreateSpace
4 out of 5 stars

Seller description: "Metal Detecting for the Beginner" is a how-to guide for anyone interested in the sport of metal detecting. Get a feel for a typical hunt; learn key terminology, and how to buy your first detector. This book guides you through the technical concepts you will need to make intelligent choices on the equipment you buy. It includes an ample list of manufacturers, suppliers, and online resources. Welcome to the wonderful world of metal detecting! Expanded 2nd edition now available.

Metal Detecting: Learning How The Easy Way!
by Ronald J. Kamrowski
Published 2011 by AuthorHouse
4.5 out of 5 stars
Seller's description: Written to share the experiences of using a metal detector. Most writings of this nature deal with the workings of a metal detector; this work contains actual events to explain that there are literally millions of places to search. Untouched areas abound in the United States where history, although only dating a few centuries, can be discovered in your own backyard. Literally thousands of unsearched sites abound in the United States alone, you can find these areas near your home to find old coins and antiques.

Magazines

There are several magazines dedicated to metal detecting and treasure hunting, with varying levels of editing and production quality. I've read most of them and subscribed to some. I think they all have value, some more than others. I think this is one of those cases where you just have to try them all and see which ones you like best.

American Digger [http://www.americandigger.com] – Published bi-monthly since January 2005, this print and digital magazine includes true accounts of relic/artifact hunting and collecting, educational and historical hints and tips, and historical recoveries from the WWII era and earlier. The publishers are detectorists themselves and are extremely accessible and responsive, and I find it one of the better edited of what's available.

Detecting365 [http://detecting365.com] – This digital-only mag bills itself as "An arsenal of metal detecting knowledge." Departments include Detecting Tips, Stories with Relics, Detecting Videos, Relic Mythbusters, Dig Details, and offers a page of Great Detecting Links.

Lost Treasure [http://www.losttreasure.com] – Billed as "the treasure hunter's guide to adventure & fortune," this mag is published monthly in print and digital format. An enthusiastic roster of writers regularly contribute articles and vibrant tales of a historical nature, and educational tips on the latest methods and equipment to find lost treasures of all types. I've subscribed for years to this mag.

Relic Hunter [http://www.relic-hunting.com] – Sadly, this digital-only mag ceased publication when publisher Jim Leonard, a much-loved figure in the treasure hunting world, passed away in 2014. At least one back issue seems to be available at issuu.com, but it's a shame they're not all there. It was a great mag.

Temerity [https://issuu.com/theodoremediallc] – This digital-only mag also appears to have ceased publication in 2013, but there are 13 issues still available to read at issuu.com.

Western & Eastern Treasures [http://www.wetreasures.com] – Published for 50 years, monthly issues are packed with adventure, excitement and the kind of inside information and ideas every treasure hunter can use to succeed. Covers coinshooting, relic hunting, beachcombing, prospecting, ghost towning, cache hunting and more. Of interest to every level of hunter, published in print and online.

Acknowledgments

No book is written by one person alone, and I have several people to thank for helping me make this one the best it could be.

I must first thank Rikki Montoro, who was the first digger to reach out to me in friendship online. Through her invitation to join her and her husband, Joe, and their digging friends from Chuck Jones' now-defunct Treasure Time forum, I learned so much about this wonderful hobby and came to feel confident enough to consider myself a real detectorist. Rikki continues to be the unofficial "hostess with the mostest" to our little clan of diggers, providing a haven of welcoming hospitality for our hunts. She and Joe most generously served as models for the front cover of this book.

Along with helping Rikki host our local gatherings, Joe Montoro is one of the most knowledgeable people I know in this hobby, generous with his knowledge yet incredibly humble about the vast repository of historical knowledge that is his brain. He has helped me understand so much about how metal detectors work and I've learned from him to be cautious about first impressions when identifying finds. I trust his judgment without reserve, and he's become one of my two "go-to guys" when I have a question about something detecting- or history-related.

The other is D.J. Yost, my great friend and best diggin' buddy. Another guy who really loves this hobby, he also is a fount of historical knowledge and accurate metal detecting information. I know when I have questions about a find, a hunting spot, or anything related to local history, I'll get the straight story and no B.S. D.J. is another digger who's really humble about his immense knowledge, and we're all lucky he shares it so freely with many others in this hobby through his blog, DJDigs.net and his Facebook page of the same name.

Because of his huge enthusiasm for metal detecting, I knew he was the guy to write the Foreword for this book, and he generously agreed to do so when I asked—I'm so grateful. He's a standup guy, a dedicated family man, and I feel blessed to count him among my best friends.

In addition to these three folks, I also surveyed some other digger friends for input on this book. Some of their tips were more advanced and so will likely appear in later guides in this series, but I still want to give a grateful shout-out to: Debbie Rosenberry Magnin, Don Hartman, Brian Mayer, Kelly Rea, and Terry Timko.

Other people I've learned from casually, either through digging with them or through online exchanges, include Drew Waholek, Ina Finn, Michael Bailey (who taught me how to make quick work of a clean plug), Tom Alexander, Dennis Amaral, Cecil "C.C." Hughes, and Richard "Gizmo" Cole.

I also want to thank Evan Granger, a fellow digger and severe weather enthusiast, from whom I've also learned some things about history and metal detecting.

Heartfelt thanks to Shelly Sickbert, who gifted me with my first two detectors, after I expressed rather often (!) my interest in giving the hobby a try.

And I can't neglect the manufacturers who make it all possible. There are many of them making great products and I don't want to slight anyone, but I must specifically thank those whose products I use and enjoy: Garrett Electronics, Inc., who manufactured my first three detectors (Treasure Ace 100, Ace 250, AT Pro); and White's Electronics, Inc., which made my latest acquisition, the Treasure Pro. I also use both of Garrett's ProPointers, and a DeteKnix Xpointer.

I would be remiss if I didn't thank every property owner who welcomed me onto their land to hunt and to dig. Where would we be without these kind and generous folks who allow us to do what we all love so much?

And I thank you, for purchasing my book and trusting that I can bring some value to your digger education.

About the Author

Mary Shafer is a fulltime freelance writer who got actively started in the metal detecting hobby in 2004. It would have been sooner, as she received her first detector as a Christmas gift in 2001, but she was unable to figure out how to get started and this book wasn't yet available to teach her how.

She lives and works in upper Bucks County, Pennsylvania, some of which has been settled since the late 1600s. This fact alone makes her area ripe for the avid metal detectorist, and indeed, some of the coins she has found since relatively early in her activity as a digger helped sharpen her interest in the pursuit.

Mary doesn't consider herself an expert digger by any stretch, but has been digging long enough to know a few helpful things while remembering her challenges getting started in the hobby. After looking around and still not seeing a beginners' guide that could be quickly digested and help newbies get out there and start swinging their detectors, she thought it was time someone wrote one. Hence, this book.

Mary is a proud member of Carla Autin's "Women Diggers" group on Facebook, where she enjoys sharing her finds and those of her fellow "dig sisters," and learning from them all.

Mary hosts her own Facebook digger page, "Metal Detecting and Treasure Hunting," at facebook.com/MetalDetectingAndTreasureHunting, and she blogs on the topic at this book's official website, Detecting101.com.

Index

Index

If you enjoyed this Quickstart Guide, we'd very much appreciate your giving it a positive review at Amazon.com. Even if you didn't love it, review it anyway. We'll see your comments and make the next one in the series better. We're a tiny little book publisher, and every review is really important to our titles getting noticed by potential readers. If you help us with your review, you're helping us be able to publish more titles like this one.

If you'd like to read this book in digital format, it's available in all major formats from Amazon.com, Kobo, Smashwords, Barnes & Noble and Apple iBooks.

Learn more about all our titles at WordForgeBooks.com. When you visit, please let us know about other books you'd like to see us publish. That's one nice thing about micro-publishers: We actually care about what you want to read, and we're far more likely to respond positively to requests.

Thanks for supporting independent publishing!

Sweet Myrrh Books

An Imprint of Word Forge Books
Riegelsville, Pennsylvania

CPSIA information can be obtained
at www.ICGtesting.com
Printed in the USA
LVOW13s1557291116
514957LV00007B/601/P